Find Your Perfect Fit

The Interactive Guide for Young Minds to Explore Dream Professions

Ekaterine Mrelashvili

Copyright ©2025EkaMrelashvili
All rights reserved.
ISBN:979-8-9926550-0-1
Published by: Amazon Kindle Direct Publishing@2025

DEDICATION

This book is dedicated to Kate. I am endlessly grateful for the joy, love, and light you bring into my life every single day. Having you as my daughter is the greatest gift.

Table of Contents

A Special Message to Kate and Young Readers	iii
Honoring Your Roots, Choosing Your Path	1
Your Unique Talents and the Magic of Genetics	3
Understanding Your Uniqueness	5
Why Finding Your Path is So Important	6
Exploring the World of Careers: Discover Your Perfect Fit	8
Envisage Your Unique Role	10
Listen to Your Inner Voice and Recognize What Excites You	12
Passion, Purpose and Real World: Finding the Balance	14
Can your dream job be different from your passion?	16
Test the Waters	17
The Right Job, the Right Vibe	18
Supercharge Your Confidence	20
From Traits to Triumph - The Key to Professional Success	21
Making Mistakes: Learning From What Goes Wrong	24
Old Jobs, New Jobs: How Work Is Always Changing	27
Role Models – Learning from the Best	30

100 + Professions, Explore the Possibilities!	33
So Many Cool Jobs Out There!	136
The Gift of Possibility	137
Find Your Purpose and Keep Going – Japanese Secrets to Stay Motivated	138
What If I Still Choose the Wrong Profession?	140
Skills, Skills, and More Skills!	141
Dream Big and You will Change the World!	142
Your Dream Profession – The Ultimate Checklist	143

A Special Message to Kate and Young Readers

There are some things we see and don't believe, and then there are the things we believe but can't yet see. Life is full of mysteries and wonders, and sometimes we can't explain why certain things happen or how they come to be. But that doesn't mean they aren't real.

10 years ago, in April 2015, on Easter morning, a little girl was born, and her name is Kate. Now, you might be wondering, what makes her so special? The truth is, Kate was a gift for me, a precious miracle I had believed in for years. She was born in a time of holy light, during the moment when the fire of Easter lit up the skies in Jerusalem. It was a time full of joy, rebirth, and the kind of magic that's hard to explain—yet here she was, my little miracle. Kate is unique. She is one of a kind. Just like you are for your parents.

Every child has their own dream story, even before they come into this world. You may not fully understand it now, but one day, you'll see how important your own story is.

Why don't you ask your parents or grandparents about the unique story of how you made your family's dreams come true? Ask them about how many people were eagerly waiting for your arrival and how happy they were to have you in their lives. You are already an incredible value to your family, a dream come true for them and you're here to be an added value to the world!

The dreams you carry inside yourself are real, and they have the power to shape your future.

Remember *The Little Prince* by Antoine de Saint-Exupéry? In that story, the Little Prince cares for a rose on his tiny planet, a rose that others might just see as ordinary. But to him, it's unique and special. He understands that while adults might focus only on what's visible on the surface, there's a deeper connection and meaning behind things that can't always be seen. Just like the Little Prince and his rose, your dreams might not always be visible to others right now, but they're there, waiting to bloom. If you believe in them and nurture them, they will grow into something extraordinary.

I've always dreamed big. Sometimes, the things I believed in were hard to believe—until they came true. So, I want to tell you something very important: believe in yourself. Believe that the dreams you carry inside are powerful and meaningful. The world may not always make sense, but if you keep following your heart and trusting in your dreams, you'll find your way.

What kind of life story will you create? What impossible thing will you choose to believe in today, and make possible tomorrow? You're here to do amazing things, big and small. No matter what dreams you have, they're already within your reach. All you need to do is take that first step.

The road ahead is yours to shape, and with belief in yourself, you can go places you never imagined. Follow your own beat and remember, there's no single way to define success, and there's no one-size-fits-all career path. It's all about finding your perfect fit—the career that aligns with your passions, talents, and interests.

The key is to stay true to yourself. Your passions will guide you toward the career that's meant for you. Finding your ideal career is like discovering your favorite song—it's a deeply personal adventure!

Honoring Your Roots, Choosing Your Path

In many cultures around the world, professions are passed down through generations. For example, in some families, becoming a doctor, teacher, or farmer is a tradition—each generation follows in the footsteps of their parents, continuing the family legacy. In countries like India, it's common for children to follow their parents' careers in business or craftsmanship, while in Italy, some family-owned businesses, such as those in food or fashion, have been passed down for centuries.

These traditions can be a source of pride and connection to family history. They provide a sense of continuity and a deep-rooted purpose, where one's work is not just a job, but a contribution to a larger family story. For many, following in these footsteps feels like an honor—keeping the family tradition alive and honoring their ancestors.

However, in today's modern world, the idea that your profession must be inherited has changed. While family traditions are still important and offer great value, young people now have more freedom than ever to choose a career based on their passions, skills, and dreams. You may love your family, respect their traditions, and appreciate the hard work they've done, but your path doesn't have to be the same as theirs.

The world is full of diverse opportunities, and choosing a profession should be about discovering what excites *you*. It's perfectly fine to honor your family's traditions while also pursuing something uniquely your own. Your roots are part of who you are, but your future is yours to shape.

Let your family's journey inspire you but remember, your profession is about finding what makes you feel alive and where your passions and strengths meet.

Sometimes, your parents or family may have ideas about what you should do or who you should be, but the most important decision is yours to make. Trust your heart, follow your dreams, and create your own story. The world is waiting for what only you can bring.

Your Unique Talents and the Magic of Genetics

You've probably heard that there is something inside you that makes you, well, *you*—a unique blend of talents, dreams, and potential that shapes your life. It's not just your personality or the way you think—it's also in your genetics! Genes are tiny instructions inside your body that help make you who you are. They decide things like your eye color, your hair type, and even the way you learn or solve problems.

Just like a recipe needs different ingredients, your genes are a mix of both your mom's and your dad's unique qualities. Sometimes, you might have talents or traits that come from one parent, like your mom's love of music or your dad's knack for fixing things. Other times, your talents may be a perfect blend of both. You may even have hidden talents waiting to be discovered!

In some cases, these talents can appear early on. For instance, Stevie Wonder was playing the piano at age six and already creating his own music by the time he was a teenager, demonstrating an extraordinary natural ability. On the flip side, talents can emerge later in life. Take Colonel Sanders, the founder of KFC, who didn't start his fried chicken business until he was 65! His passion for cooking and entrepreneurship took time to develop, but when it did, it led to massive success.

Parents often recognize these little talents early on, noticing that you might have a special gift for something—maybe you're a natural at drawing, singing, or building things. These gifts are part of the genetic recipe that makes you, *you*. Your parents, grandparents see the unique traits and strengths from both sides of the family, and they'll encourage you to explore and develop them.

No matter where your talents come from, they are yours to shape and grow. Your genes might help guide you, but what you do with them is up to you. So, embrace what makes you different, explore all the possibilities, and remember, your talents are part of what makes you truly special.

Understanding Your Uniqueness

Have you ever noticed how no two people are exactly the same? It's like a garden with all kinds of flowers. Some people are like vibrant sunflowers, others are like delicate roses, and some are like wild daisies—simple, but full of charm. Each person adds something unique to the mix. So do you. You are your own limited edition—there's no one else like you, and that's pretty awesome!

You might not know it yet, but there are things you do better than anyone else. Maybe you can make the best pancake stack, or maybe you're a pro at picking out the perfect birthday card. Maybe you're great at making people laugh when they need it most. Whatever it is, your special gifts are what make you—you! And the world? Well, the world needs exactly what only you can offer.

There's no need to try to be like someone else. You're not a copy machine, you're a masterpiece in your own right! Imagine if everyone tried to be exactly the same—how boring would that be? The world needs you to be YOU, in all your quirky, wonderful, unique glory.

Why Finding Your Path is So Important

Let's take a moment to think about finding your place in the world. Picture it like a game of musical chairs. The music stops, and you have to find your chair. Here's the challenge: there are a lot of chairs, but only one that fits you perfectly. No need to stress though—if you miss a chair, just get up, keep moving, and try again!

Finding your place in life is a bit like that. It's all about discovering where you fit, where your heart feels the most alive, and where you can really shine. And no, you don't have to have it all figured out by the time you're 10. It's okay to wander a bit, try different things, and even trip over a few chairs along the way. That's how you learn!

Why does it matter to find your place? Well, think about it like this: if you don't know where you belong, you might end up sitting on the floor instead of in the comfy chair you deserve. But when you find that perfect spot, everything just clicks. You'll feel like you're exactly where you're supposed to be, and suddenly, the world feels like a way better place to be part of.

It doesn't matter if your place looks different from someone else's. That's the beauty of life! You get to decide what makes you happy, what makes you jump out of bed in the morning (besides your breakfast), and how you want to make your mark on the world. If someone else's dream looks cooler or seems easier, remember that your dream is just as cool—and it's uniquely yours.

Even when things feel confusing or you don't know what comes next, trust that the perfect "chair" will be waiting for you when the music stops. And when you find it, you're going to feel like you're in the right place, ready to take on the world with everything you've got.

The best part is that you're already on your way—one step at a time, just like every other unique, amazing person in this big, beautiful world. And don't forget: the world is way more fun when we all bring our special, quirky selves to the party. Go ahead, be you!

Exploring the World of Careers: Discover Your Perfect Fit

Have you ever looked at someone and thought, "Wow, that job looks so cool! I want to do that!" Maybe it was a veterinarian taking care of cute puppies, or a scientist discovering things about space that no one else has ever seen. Or maybe you thought, "I could totally be the first person to invent a snack that tastes like pizza *and* ice cream!"

The world is full of so many professions, and the fun part is, you don't have to stick to just one right now. In fact, you shouldn't! The best part about being young is that you have all the time in the world to try out different things and see what lights you up. The world is your playground, and there are literally endless options.

From being a teacher to a designer, an astronaut to a chef, a writer to an engineer, you have all the tools to explore what the world has to offer. And it's important to explore as many different paths as you can, because the more you learn about what's out there, the easier it will be to figure out what's right for you.

It's like going to an all-you-can-eat buffet. At first, you might want to try a little bit of everything—pasta, sushi, some mystery dish that you don't know the name of, but it looks good. After trying a little of everything, you'll know exactly what you *really* like and what maybe isn't your thing.

Start exploring! Ask questions. Look around. Dive into activities that let you see how different professions work. You might be surprised by what you end up loving. Who knows? Maybe the next time you see a firefighter, you'll think, "I could totally save the day in a fire truck!" Or maybe you'll see a designer creating amazing clothes and realize, "That's it. I want to make people look and feel awesome!"

Envisage Your Unique Role

When you've got all these cool professions floating in your mind, here's the fun part: imagining the role you would love to play in the world. I know, I know—it's a *big* question, but don't worry. You don't need all the answers right away. You can start by thinking about what excites you, what you're good at, and what you *really* enjoy doing.

Think of your dreams as little clues guiding you toward your role. Maybe you love solving puzzles—could that mean you're a future detective or an engineer? Or maybe you're always the one organizing events for your friends—does that mean you're a future event planner or a project manager? There's no limit to what you can do, so let your imagination run wild!

A great way to start imagining your future is by asking yourself a few fun questions:

- What makes me excited? Is it helping others? Creating things? Exploring new places?
- What hobbies do I love? Could one of them turn into a job I would enjoy?
- If I could wake up tomorrow and do anything at all, what would it be?
- Why do certain places or environments make me feel happy or inspired?

And here's the most important thing to remember: whatever role you imagine for yourself doesn't have to be "perfect." It doesn't have to be the most popular job or the one everyone else thinks is cool. What matters is that it makes *you* feel excited and passionate. You could be a fashion designer in the morning, an inventor in the afternoon, and a superhero at night. There's no limit to the roles you can play in the world.

Your dream role is like an adventure waiting for you to discover. You just need to start imagining it, even if you don't know all the details yet. The world will give you the tools you need—whether it's books, experiences, or conversations with people who have cool jobs—to help you figure it out. So, keep dreaming big and stay curious!

Listen to Your Inner Voice and Recognize What Excites You

Okay, so you're out there exploring your passions, and you're having fun. But how do you know which direction to go in? How do you figure out what's really calling you? Here's the thing: inside you is a little voice (I promise it's there, even if it's a bit quiet sometimes). This voice is your inner guide. It knows what excites you, what you're good at, and what will bring you joy. The tricky part is learning how to listen to it.

When that voice speaks, it's usually the one that says things like, "Hey, I'd really love to try that!" or, "This feels right, I think I'm onto something!" It might sound a little different for each person, but it always has your best interests in mind. And don't worry, you won't hear it like a megaphone; it's more like a gentle whisper. When you get a hunch to try something new, or you feel extra happy doing something you never expected, that's probably your inner voice giving you a high-five!

The more you listen to this voice, the easier it gets to recognize what truly excites you. Trust me, once you start tuning in, you'll start to notice what makes you feel alive—whether it's playing music, building things, or even helping others with their dreams.

And here's the most important thing: whatever excites you is worth pursuing. Maybe it's a small passion right now, but if you keep following that spark, it might turn into something amazing. So, listen closely, and when your inner voice says, "Let's try this," say "Yes!" and go for it. Imagine you're at the beginning of an epic adventure. You have a backpack filled with possibilities (don't forget your sense of curiosity). The road ahead is full of twists, turns, and maybe even a few bumps, but every step is a chance to discover more about yourself. You might not have all the answers today, but don't worry—no one does! In fact, the fun part is figuring it all out as you go along. Think of every experience, every conversation, and every random new hobby you try as a clue that gets you closer to understanding what you truly love.

Self-discovery isn't something that happens overnight. Don't rush it. The best discoveries happen when you're not looking for them. So, take your time and enjoy the process. You're allowed to experiment, try new things, and even change your mind a million times. That's how you find out who you really are.

Passion, Purpose and Real World: Finding the Balance

Let's talk about something really important: balance. Finding the right fit isn't just about doing what sounds fun—it's about making sure it matches what you're good at and works in the real world. It's about combining your passion, your skills, and the practical needs of the world around you. When you find that balance, you'll be on the path to something that works for you and the world.

Ask yourself these questions:

- What am I good at? (Your skills are like your superpowers!)
- What do I love doing? (Your passion is the energy that makes you want to jump out of bed every day!)
- Can this actually work in the real world? (Is it something people need, or something you can really do?)
- What do people always ask for your help with?
- What comes easy to you that others might find tricky?
- What is my bigger purpose in all this?

When you can balance all three—what you love, what you're good at, and what makes sense in the real world—you're on the right track!

Can your dream job be different from your passion?

Absolutely! While your passion is something you love doing, like drawing, playing sports, or baking, your dream job might be something that doesn't match exactly but still excites you. For example, you might love playing video games but dream of being a game designer or programmer, or you might have a passion for animals but want to become a teacher instead of a vet.

Your dream job doesn't always have to be the same as your passion, and that's okay! Sometimes, the skills needed for your passion might be different from what's needed in your dream job, or your passion might be something that's hard to turn into a full-time career.

The key is to find a balance—if your dream job doesn't line up with your passion, you can still keep your passion alive as a hobby or side project while working at a job that excites you in different ways. You can enjoy both your job and your passions, and sometimes mixing the two can lead to a career that's even more fun than you imagined!

Test the Waters

Here's the best part: you don't have to know everything right now! Finding your fit means trying things out. Ever dipped your toes in the water before jumping into the pool? That's exactly what you need to do with your future! The more you explore, the clearer things will become.

Want to know if a job really feels right? Try it out! You don't need to dive straight into a full-time career just yet. Here are a few fun ways to test the waters:

- Internships: Even a small internship can give you a taste of what a job is really like. You'll learn a ton and get a sneak peek into the world of work!

- Hobbies: Some of the things you love doing as a hobby might actually be something you could do professionally one day. Whether it's drawing, coding, or even baking cupcakes—what you enjoy doing in your free time could lead to something amazing!

- Shadowing: Spend a day (or more!) shadowing someone who's doing the job you're curious about. Watching them in action can help you see if it's something you'd enjoy doing too!

- Volunteering: Another great way to try out different jobs and help others while learning new skills. You can explore areas like teaching, event planning, or even working with animals—all while making a difference!

Go ahead—dip your toes in, try things out, and trust your gut. You might just find that one job that makes you want to jump in and swim with excitement!

The Right Job, the Right Vibe

Choosing a profession is a lot like choosing friends. Just like you want to be around people who make you feel comfortable, happy, and supported, you want to find a job that makes you feel the same way. Some friends bring out the best in you, while others might not fit as well with your personality or interests. Similarly, the best profession for you is the one that feels right and matches your skills, interests, and values.

When choosing friends, you might notice you feel more comfortable with people who think like you, share similar hobbies, or understand your sense of humor. The same goes for professions. You want to find a job that feels natural, one where you can use your strengths and do things you enjoy. You wouldn't want to force a friendship with someone who doesn't understand you or make you feel happy—and you shouldn't force yourself into a job that doesn't bring you joy or match your abilities.

Just like with friendships, it's important to spend time exploring different professions to find the one that clicks with you. Some might be a perfect fit right away, while others might take some time to get to know. But when you find the right one, it will feel like finding a friend who truly understands you.

So, when thinking about your career, remember that it's about finding your "work friends," the people, skills, and experiences that will make you feel valued, excited, and ready to grow.

Supercharge Your Confidence

Confidence is key to unlocking your full potential. You've already got the skills, but to truly shine, you need to believe in yourself. No matter how awesome your superpowers are, it's important to believe in them! Confidence isn't something you're born with - it's something you can build, one step at a time.

- Celebrate Your Wins: big or small, every victory counts! Whether you finish a project or help a friend, take a moment to appreciate your achievements.

- Practice, Practice, Practice: the more you practice something, the more confident you become. Whether it's speaking in front of the class or playing the piano, practice is the secret to success!

- Positive Self-Talk: whenever you feel unsure, remind yourself of all the awesome things you've already done. Say it with me: "I am capable. I am strong. I believe in myself!"

Reflection – Your Superpowers:

- What are my top three superpowers?
- Which superpower do I want to develop even more?
- How can I share my superpowers with others?

From Traits to Triumph - The Key to Professional Success

In every job, your personality and skills play a huge role in how successful you are. It's not just about what you know or how smart you are - it's about the unique traits you bring to the table. Whether you want to be a doctor, a teacher, a designer, or anything else, certain qualities and abilities will help you stand out and succeed in your career.
Let's begin with some of the key personal skills and traits that are important in almost every profession.

Communication is one of the most important skills you'll need. Whether you're talking to coworkers, customers, or your boss, clear communication helps you express your ideas, listen to others, and build strong relationships. It ensures everyone understands each other and works together smoothly.
Kindness and **empathy** are qualities that make a huge difference in any job. Being kind helps build trust, while empathy allows you to understand others' feelings and collaborate better. Imagine working in a place where everyone is supportive and understanding—it would make teamwork much easier and more enjoyable.
Confidence is another key trait. It helps you believe in yourself and your abilities, which is crucial when you're taking on challenges. Leadership is related to confidence but doesn't always mean being the boss. Leadership is about motivating others, making good decisions, and guiding your team to success.
Curiosity also plays a huge role in any profession. Being curious means you're always learning and exploring new ideas. It helps you think outside the box and find creative solutions to problems. Curious people never stop growing—they seek out new information, which helps them stay ahead in their careers.
Creativity is one of the most essential skills in today's world. It's not just for artists or designers; it's crucial for problem-solving and innovation in every profession. Creativity helps you think beyond the obvious, develop new ideas, and solve problems in unique ways. It allows you to approach challenges from different angles and find solutions others might miss.
Discipline is another critical skill. It's about staying focused on your work, following through with tasks, and sticking to your commitments. Discipline keeps you organized, helps you stay on track, and ensures you don't get distracted. Without it, you may struggle to meet deadlines or complete tasks to the best of your ability, but with it, you remain focused and steady as you move forward in your career.
Problem-solving is an indispensable skill. Whether you're solving a tricky issue or coming up with new strategies, the ability to analyze problems and

find solutions is essential. Problem-solving also ties into creativity, as it involves thinking critically and finding new ways to overcome obstacles.
Teamwork is necessary for almost every job. Being able to work well with others, share ideas, and combine strengths helps you achieve common goals. Great teamwork leads to a positive working environment, where everyone feels valued and supported.

In addition to these personal traits and key skills, there are also important soft skills—the ones that might not be taught in school but are vital in the real world. One of the most important soft skills is **emotional intelligence**. This is the ability to manage your own emotions and understand others' emotions. It helps you stay calm under pressure, build positive relationships, and deal with stress in a healthy way.

In every job, your personality and skills can play a huge role in how successful you are. It's not just about what you know or how smart you are—it's about the unique traits you bring to the table. Whether you want to be a doctor, a teacher, a designer, or anything else, certain qualities and abilities will help you stand out and succeed in your career.

As you look ahead to your future career, remember that **what you do is important, but how you do it matters just as much.** Your personality, your kindness, and your ability to work with others can help set you apart and make you successful in any profession. Start thinking about how you can develop your skills and grow your strengths.

Making Mistakes: Learning From What Goes Wrong

Recently, one book became a bestseller with a surprising title: *How to Make Mistakes* (by Dr. Laura Kelly). Sounds weird, right? But the truth is, making mistakes is a big part of learning and growing! Everyone makes mistakes, whether you're trying out a new sport, learning how to play an instrument, or figuring out what job you might want in the future. The important thing is not to be afraid of them. In fact, mistakes are a huge part of the process that helps you improve and get better at whatever you're doing.

Making a mistake doesn't mean you've failed—it just means you've learned something new. It's like when you're building a puzzle. If you try to put a piece in the wrong spot, you learn that it doesn't fit there, and then you can try a different place. The same happens with anything you try.

Every time you mess up, you're one step closer to getting it right. The more mistakes you make, the more you discover what works and what doesn't.

For example, maybe you've tried something and didn't get it right the first time, like a science experiment or a school project. Instead of getting upset, think about what you can learn from the mistake. Maybe you can ask questions, practice more, or try a new strategy next time. Mistakes help you figure out the best ways to do things, and they teach you how to keep going even when things don't go as planned.

The most successful people in the world? They've made tons of mistakes! But here's the key: they didn't let those mistakes stop them. They learned from them, made changes, and kept trying until they reached their goals. Making mistakes builds your resilience, which is like a superpower that helps you bounce back even stronger.

The more you try and learn from mistakes, the better you become at overcoming challenges.

Next time you make a mistake, don't think of it as something bad. Think of it as a step on the path to becoming better at whatever you're doing. Remember, everyone makes mistakes—it's how you deal with them that makes all the difference. Keep going, keep trying, and know that mistakes are just part of the adventure on the way to success!

To explore some amazing mistake stories, you can dive deeper into how mistakes turned into some of the most famous discoveries and inventions in history. Whether it's how the Leaning Tower of Pisa became a world landmark due to an architectural error, or how an accidental mold led to the life-saving discovery of penicillin, each of these cases shows that mistakes aren't always the end—they can be the beginning of something great.

Sometimes the best discoveries happen when things don't go as planned!

Old Jobs, New Jobs: How Work Is Always Changing

Professions have been around for as long as people have needed jobs to survive and thrive. The history of professions is a story of change, adaptation, and sometimes even disappearance. Over time, as societies grow, technology advances, and people's needs change, some jobs are born, some evolve, and others are left behind.

Long ago, many professions were tied to basic survival. For example, people needed farmers to grow food, blacksmiths to make tools, and weavers to create clothes. Those jobs were vital, and people trained for them in their families or communities. Some of those early jobs still exist today, like farmers, but they've changed a lot. Farmers now use big machines, GPS, and computers instead of using only their hands and basic tools.

As societies grew more complex, new professions were born. In ancient Egypt, scribes were one of the most important professions. They could read and write, which was a rare skill. Scribes helped record history and kept important documents safe. Imagine how much power you'd have if you were one of the few who could read and write! But not all professions stick around forever. Over time, new technology or changes in society can make old jobs disappear. For example, the profession of town crier was once common. A town crier was a person who went around town shouting the news because not everyone could read or had access to newspapers. Today, we get news from the internet, TV, and phones, so the job of a town crier is no longer needed.

Another example is the lamplighter. In the past, before electric streetlights, a lamplighter's job was to light gas lamps in the streets at night and snuff them out in the morning. Today, streetlights are automatic, so lamplighters have disappeared.

Some professions have been replaced by machines. Elevator operator used to be a common job in tall buildings, guiding the elevator to the right floor. Now, elevators are automatic, and you simply press a button to get to your floor.

But it's not just old jobs that disappear; new ones are always being created. In today's world, jobs like social media manager, app developer, and video game designer didn't exist just a few decades ago! The rise of the internet and new technology has made these professions possible.

As we look at the history of professions, we realize that the world is always changing, and so are the jobs people do today. Some jobs fade away, but others evolve and grow. For example, many jobs in the medical field have changed with new technology, and while there might be fewer blacksmiths now, there are plenty of engineers and designers working with metals and materials in different ways.

What's amazing is that YOU could be the one to create a job that doesn't even exist yet. As technology and ideas keep growing, new opportunities will open that we can't even imagine right now. So, as you think about your future profession, remember: professions can come and go, but what's most important is finding something you're passionate about—and who knows, maybe you'll help invent the next big job that everyone will want!

Role Models – Learning from the Best

Have you ever wondered how famous people found their dream jobs? What made them decide to become the people they are today? In this chapter, we're going to look at some inspiring people who followed their passions and turned them into successful careers.

Albert Einstein – The Curious Thinker
Albert Einstein is known for his brilliant mind and famous theory of relativity, but he didn't always know he would become a scientist. As a child, he loved to ask questions and solve problems. He was curious about how things worked and often wondered about the mysteries of the world. Einstein didn't get everything right at first, but he kept trying. His curiosity and determination led him to become one of the greatest scientists in history. Just like Einstein, you can use your curiosity to explore your interests and figure out what excites you.

Oprah Winfrey – The Talk Show Legend
Oprah Winfrey's story is a powerful example of following your heart. She started out working in TV news but realized her passion was in connecting with people and sharing their stories. Oprah worked hard, faced many challenges, and never gave up on her dream to make people feel heard. Her dedication and empathy for others led her to become one of the most famous talk show hosts in the world. She teaches us that when you're doing something that feels meaningful to you, amazing things can happen.

Steve Jobs – The Tech Innovator
Steve Jobs was the founder of Apple and changed the way we use technology today. But his journey wasn't easy! He didn't always fit in at school and even got kicked out of college. However, he never stopped believing in his ideas. He was passionate about creating things that could make people's lives better, and he loved using his creativity to solve problems. His story shows us that sometimes the road to success is full of twists and turns, but passion and persistence can lead you to amazing places.

J.K. Rowling – The Creator of Harry Potter
Before J.K. Rowling became the world-famous author of the *Harry Potter* series, she faced many challenges. She was a single mother struggling to make ends meet, and she had a lot of rejections before her books were published. But she kept writing because she loved storytelling. She turned her passion for writing into a career that has inspired millions of kids and adults around

the world. J.K. Rowling's story shows us that following your passion, even when things get tough, can lead to great things!

Malala Yousafzai – The Brave Advocate for Education
Malala Yousafzai is a true hero. When she was young, she spoke out about the importance of girls' education, even when it was dangerous. Despite facing huge challenges and obstacles, Malala never stopped believing in her cause. She became the youngest-ever Nobel Prize laureate because of her bravery and commitment to making the world a better place for girls. Malala's story teaches us that no matter how young you are, you can make a huge difference if you stand up for what you believe in.

What Can We Learn from These Role Stories?
These famous people didn't just sit around waiting for their dream jobs to find them. They had to work hard, be brave, and follow their passions—even when it wasn't easy. They made mistakes, faced challenges, and kept going. You can do the same!

- Be curious: Just like Einstein, ask questions and never stop exploring the world around you.
- Follow your heart: Oprah's story reminds us that following what feels right to you can lead to amazing opportunities.
- Stay determined: Like Steve Jobs, you may face setbacks, but don't give up on your ideas or passions.
- Keep believing in yourself: J.K. Rowling showed us it's okay to fail and be rejected—just keep going and keep believing in your dreams.
- Stand up for what's right: Malala's courage teaches us that you can make a big difference by standing up for what you believe in.

Reflect on someone who inspires you—whether it's a famous figure, a family member, or a friend. What do you admire about them? Consider the qualities they demonstrate and how those traits contribute to their success. Remember, you have your own unique strengths and the ability to pursue your dreams. With a clear goal and determination, you can make a meaningful impact in your own way!

100 + Professions, Explore the Possibilities!

Welcome to the *Professions Interactive Pages!* This is your chance to dive deep into a world full of exciting, creative, and even some unusual careers. Over the next pages, you will explore about 100 different professions—some you might already know well and others that might seem a little weird, but no matter, every profession has something unique to offer. The interesting thing is that you can do *any* of these professions, but here's the key: while considering each one, you'll notice that some will feel like they fit well, and others will feel like they fit *perfectly* with your personality and abilities. And that's the purpose of this book—to help you find your *best fit*.

As you explore each profession, you'll answer questions and think about what excites you and what feels right. You'll learn about your preferences, your strengths, and what sparks your curiosity. At the end of each page, you'll get to ask yourself: Could this be *your* dream job?

You might even find that your thoughts and ideas change as you grow. That's perfectly fine! You can always come back to this journal in a year or two, reflect on what you wrote, and maybe discover that new interests or talents have emerged. Keep exploring, stay curious, and don't be afraid to dream big—because your perfect fit might still be waiting for you.

Let's get started! Turn the page and begin your adventure into the world of professions. Who knows? Your future profession could be one page away!

1. ASTRONAUT

An astronaut is a scientist, engineer and explorer who journeys into space to study planets, stars, and conduct experiments in zero gravity. Their work helps us understand space, improve technology, and explore life beyond Earth. They work on spacecrafts, space stations, and sometimes even walk on the Moon or Mars!

Your Mission – Imagine You're an astronaut!

Zero Gravity Fun! Imagine floating in space. What would you explore first on the spaceship?

Planet Exploration You've landed on a new planet! What might you discover? Draw or describe a new alien or landmark.

Tools for the Job What futuristic gadgets would help you explore space?

A Day in Space What would your schedule look like on the International Space Station? What tasks would you do?

Dream Space Mission If you could visit any destination in space, where would you go? The Moon, Mars, or beyond?

Skills for Success What skills are important for astronauts? Think about teamwork, problem-solving, and staying calm.

Talk to an Astronaut – Stay Curious

If you could ask an astronaut anything, what would it be? (It's a great idea to try to find one!) Speaking with a professional can give you amazing insights into their world. Here are a few fun questions to spark your imagination:

"What's the coolest thing you've seen in space?" or "What's the hardest part of living in space?" or "What do you miss most about Earth?"

Bonus Activity

Explore stories of astronauts who've traveled to space. Ask your teacher or librarian for book or movie recommendations and write them down here.

Books:

Movies:

Rate This Profession

On a scale of 1 (not interested) to 10 (dream job), how well does this profession suit your personality and interests?

1 2 3 4 5 6 7 8 9 10

2. VETERINARIAN

A veterinarian is a medical professional who cares for animals, diagnosing, treating, and preventing illnesses or injuries in pets, farm animals, and wild creatures.

Your Mission - Imagine You're a veterinarian!

Animal Care Imagine a pet or farm animal comes for a checkup. What's the first thing you'd do?

Wildlife Adventure You're helping wild animals in their natural habitat. What animals would you encounter?

The Vet's Toolbox What medical tools would you use in your practice, from stethoscopes to X-ray machines?

A Day in the Life What does a typical day as a vet look like? Do you see pets, assist in surgeries, or work with farm animals?

Dream Job If you could work with any animal, which one would it be?

Skills for Success What skills are important to be a successful vet? Think about compassion, calmness in emergencies, and communication.

Talk to a Veterinarian – Stay Curious

If you could ask a veterinarian anything, what would it be? Here are a few questions to spark your imagination: "What's the most rewarding part of being a vet?" or "What's the hardest part of working with animals?" or "Do animals ever surprise you with their personalities?"

Bonus Activity

Explore stories about veterinarians. Ask your teacher or librarian for book or movie recommendations.

Books:

Movies:

Rate This Profession
On a scale of 1 (not interested) to 10 (dream job),
how well does this profession suit your personality and interests?
1 2 3 4 5 6 7 8 9 10

3. ARTIST

An artist is a creative person who expresses themselves through art forms like painting, drawing, sculpture, photography, or digital art. They use their imagination and skills to create works that evoke emotion, tell stories, or inspire others. Their art can be found in galleries, museums, streets, or online.

Your Mission – Imagine you're an artist!

Creating Your Masterpiece Imagine you're in your studio, ready to create. What medium would you use—paint, sketches, or maybe photography? What would your subject be?

Artistic Inspiration You're at an art gallery. What piece catches your eye—an iconic painting, a sculpture, or a mural? What type of art inspires you?

The Artist's Tools What tools would you need? Brushes, clay, paint, or digital tools?

A Day on the job What would your day look like working on a big project? Would you spend time in your studio, or perhaps sell your work at an event?

Dream Art Project If you could create any artwork, what would it be? A mural, sculpture, or a collection of paintings telling a story?

Skills for Success What skills are key for artists? Creativity, patience, drawing, or expressing emotions through your work?

Talk to an Artist – Stay Curious If you could ask an artist anything, what would it be? Here are a few questions to spark your imagination: "What inspires your artwork?" or "What's the most challenging part of being an artist?"

Bonus Activity

Explore stories about artists. Ask your teacher or librarian for book or movie recommendations.

Books:

Movies:

Rate This Profession

On a scale of 1 (not interested) to 10 (dream job), how well does this profession suit your personality and interests?

1 2 3 4 5 6 7 8 9 10

4. TEACHER

A teacher helps students learn and grow, creating lessons, guiding them through subjects, and inspiring curiosity. Teachers shape the future by helping students build skills, knowledge, and confidence to succeed.

Your Mission – Imagine you're a teacher!

Classroom Setup Imagine you're teaching a new lesson. How would you start—explaining a math problem, reading a story, or setting up an experiment?

Teaching Moment You helped a student understand something difficult. How does it feel to see their excitement when they get it?

The Teacher's Tools What kind of tools would you need to teach? Books, whiteboards, lesson plans, or maybe fun decorations?

A Day in the Life What does a typical day look like in your classroom? What activities would you plan and how would you interact with students?

Dream Classroom If you could design your perfect classroom, what would it include—reading corners, learning stations, or colorful artwork?

Skills for Success What skills are important for a successful teacher? Patience, creativity, communication, and a love for helping others learn?

Talk to a Teacher – Stay Curious

If you could ask a teacher anything, what would it be? Here are a few questions to spark your imagination: "What's the most rewarding part of teaching?" or "How do you make learning fun?" or "What's the biggest challenge you face?"

Bonus Activity

Explore stories about teachers. Ask your teacher or librarian for book or movie recommendations.

Books:

Movies:

Rate This Profession

On a scale of 1 (not interested) to 10 (dream job), how well does this profession suit your personality and interests?

1   2   3   4   5   6   7   8   9   10

5. FIREFIGHTER

A firefighter is a hero who saves lives and protects property from fires and emergencies. They fight fires, perform rescues, and educate the public on fire safety. The job requires bravery, teamwork, and quick thinking.

Your Mission – Imagine you're a firefighter!

The Fire Rescue What's the first thing you'd do when you arrive at a fire? Help people escape, fight the flames, or assist your team?

Rescue Time! How would you stay calm and rescue someone from a burning building?

The Firefighter's Gear What gear would you need—heavy uniforms, oxygen tanks, powerful hoses? What's most important?

A Day on the Job What would your day at the fire station look like—responding to emergencies, training, or checking equipment?

Dream Rescue Mission What emergency would you want to respond to—fire, flood, earthquake? Why?

Skills for Success Important skills include physical strength, quick thinking, and knowledge of specialized equipment.

Talk to a Firefighter – Stay Curious

If you had the chance to talk to a firefighter, what would you ask them? (It's a great idea to try to find one!) Speaking with a professional can give you amazing insights into their world.

Here are some ideas to get you started: "What's the hardest part of being a firefighter?" or "How do you stay calm during a dangerous rescue?" or "What's your most memorable experience on the job?"

Bonus Activity

To get inspired, explore stories about firefighters. Ask your teacher or librarian for book or movie recommendations.

Books:

Movies:

Rate This Profession

On a scale of 1 (not interested) to 10 (dream job), how well does this profession suit your personality and interests?

1   2   3   4   5   6   7   8   9   10

6. SCIENTIST

A scientist explores the world by asking big questions and finding answers through research and experiments. They study everything from tiny particles to the universe, using curiosity to make discoveries, solve problems, and improve our understanding of the world.

Your Mission Imagine you're a scientist!

Experiment Time Imagine you're in a lab, conducting an experiment. What would you study—plants, animals, chemicals, or maybe space?

Scientific Discovery You've made an amazing discovery! What is it, and how do you feel about unlocking a scientific mystery?

The Scientist's Tools What tools would you need for your work—microscopes, test tubes, computers, or even space telescopes?

A Day in the Life What would your day look like as a scientist? Would you be in a lab, exploring nature, or writing up findings? How would you collaborate with other scientists?

Dream Scientific Discovery If you could make any discovery, what would it be—discovering a new planet, inventing medicine, or solving a nature mystery?

Skills for Success What skills are important to be a successful scientist? Curiosity, problem-solving, and focus for long hours on complex problems?

Talk to a Scientist – Stay Curious If you could ask a scientist anything, what would you ask? Here are a few fun questions to spark your imagination: "What's the most exciting part of being a scientist?" or "What's the biggest challenge in your research?" or "How do you stay curious when working on tough problems?"

Bonus Activity

Explore stories about scientists and their discoveries. Ask your teacher or librarian for book or movie recommendations.

Books:

Movies:

Rate This Profession

On a scale of 1 (not interested) to 10 (dream job), how well does this profession suit your personality and interests?

1   2   3   4   5   6   7   8   9   10

7. MUSICIAN

A musician creates and performs music, using instruments, their voice, or technology to express emotions, tell stories, and connect with people. Musicians play various roles, from composers to performers, across genres, such as classical, jazz, pop, or rock.

Your Mission Imagine you're a musician!

Instrument Time What instrument would you play—guitar, piano, drums, or your voice?

Musical Creation You've written a song! What's it about, and how does it make you feel?

The Musician's Tools What tools do you need—musical instruments, sheet music, or sound equipment?

A Day in the Life What would your day look like—performing, composing, or recording? How do you collaborate with other musicians?

Dream Performance If you could perform anywhere, where would it be—on stage, in a recording studio, or at a music festival?

Skills for Success What skills are important for a successful musician? Creativity, discipline, and the ability to work with others?

Talk to a Musician – Stay Curious If you could ask a musician anything, what would it be? Here are some ideas to get you started: "What's your favorite part of performing?" or "How do you overcome creative blocks?" or "What's the most challenging part of being a musician?"

Bonus Activity

Explore music from different genres and cultures. Ask your teacher or librarian for recommendations!

Books:

Movies:

Rate This Profession

On a scale of 1 (not interested) to 10 (dream job), how well does this profession suit your personality and interests?

1 2 3 4 5 6 7 8 9 10

8. DOCTOR

A doctor is a medical professional who helps people stay healthy, treats illnesses and diagnoses diseases. Doctors work in hospitals, clinics, or private practices, sometimes specializing in areas like pediatrics, surgery, or cardiology.

Your Mission Imagine you're a doctor!

Diagnosing the Problem What symptoms would you look for to diagnose an illness?

The Treatment Plan You've diagnosed your patient's condition. What treatment would you suggest? Would you prescribe medicine, recommend surgery, or provide physical therapy?

Doctor's Tools What tools would you use to diagnose and treat patients? Think about stethoscopes, thermometers, medical tests, or surgical tools.

A Day in the Life of a Doctor What does your day look like—seeing patients, doing surgery, or reviewing test results?

Dream Specialization

If you could specialize, what would it be—pediatrics, surgery, or may be family medicine?

Skills for Success What skills are important for a successful doctor? Empathy, problem-solving, medical knowledge, and the ability to stay calm in emergencies?

Talk to a Doctor – Stay Curious If you could ask a doctor anything, what would you ask? Maybe, "What's the most rewarding part of being a doctor?" or "How do you deal with difficult cases?" or "What advice do you have for future doctors?"

Bonus Activity

Explore stories about doctors. Ask your teacher or librarian for book or movie recommendations!

Books:

Movies:

Rate This Profession

On a scale of 1 (not interested) to 10 (dream job), how well does this profession suit your personality and interests?

1 2 3 4 5 6 7 8 9 10

9. CHEF

A chef is a professional who prepares food, manages kitchens, and creates meals. Chefs work in restaurants, hotels, and catering services, specializing in various cuisines like Italian, French, or sushi. They aim to create delicious and visually appealing dishes that bring joy to people.

Your Mission Imagine you're a chef!

Menu Creation Imagine you're designing a menu. What types of dishes would you serve? Comfort food, healthy meals, or gourmet dishes?

The Perfect Dish What's your signature dish, and what does it look, smell, and taste like?

Chef's Tools What tools are essential for cooking? Knives, spatulas, blenders, or special grills?

A Day in the Life of a Chef What does your day look like in a busy kitchen? Chopping vegetables, managing staff, or tasting sauces?

Dream Restaurant If you could open a restaurant, what type of food would you serve—bakery, sushi, or comfort food truck?

Skills for Success What skills are important for a successful chef? Creativity, pressure management, and attention to detail?

Talk to an Expert – Stay Curious If you could ask a chef anything, what would you ask? Maybe, "What's your favorite dish to cook and why?" or "How do you handle stress in the kitchen?" or "What advice would you give to aspiring chefs?"

Bonus Activity
Explore stories about famous chefs and their paths to success. Ask your teacher or librarian for recommendations!
Books:

Movies:

Rate This Profession
On a scale of 1 (not interested) to 10 (dream job),
how well does this profession suit your personality and interests?
1   2   3   4   5   6   7   8   9   10

10. ENGINEER

An engineer is a problem-solver who designs, builds, and improves things to make the world better. Engineers work in fields like construction, technology, and aerospace using math, science, and creativity to solve real-world problems. They create innovations such as bridges, new technologies, and eco-friendly buildings.

>**Your Mission** – Imagine you're an engineer!
>
>**Design Your Dream Invention** What would your invention be? A robot, a new car, or a helpful machine?
>
>**Problem-Solving Challenge** How would you solve a tough problem? Brainstorm, work in teams, or run experiments?
>
>**Engineer's Tools** What tools would you need—computers, blueprints, 3D printers, or big construction machines?
>
>**A Day in the Life of an Engineer** What would your workday look like—designing, testing, or overseeing projects?
>
>**Dream Engineering Project** What would your dream project be—designing a spaceship, building a city, or creating new transportation?
>
>**Skills for Success** What skills are key for engineers—problem-solving, teamwork, math, science, and creativity?
>
>**Talk to an Engineer – Stay Curious** If you could ask an engineer anything, what would it be? You can try: "What's the most exciting project you've worked on?" or "What challenges do you face in your work?" or "What advice would you give someone who wants to become an engineer?"

Bonus Activity
Explore stories about famous engineers. Ask your teacher or librarian for recommendations!
Books:

Movies:

Rate This Profession
On a scale of 1 (not interested) to 10 (dream job), how well does this profession suit your personality and interests?

1 2 3 4 5 6 7 8 9 10

11. AUTHOR

An author is a storyteller who creates books, articles, or stories to entertain, inform, or inspire others. Authors use their imagination and writing skills to craft narratives in genres like fiction, non-fiction, poetry, or even scripts. They bring characters and worlds to life through words, connecting with readers through their creativity.

Your Mission Imagine you're an author!

Create a Story What would your story be about—adventure, mystery, or drama? How do you want readers to feel?

Character Creation Who are your main characters and what makes them unique?

Author's Tools What tools would you use—pen, computer, or voice recordings? What's most important for telling your story?

A Day in the Life of an Author What would your writing routine look like—working on a novel, editing or brainstorming ideas?

Dream Book What kind of book would you write—a bestseller, children's book, or philosophical novel?

Skills for Success Creativity, dedication, discipline and the ability to connect with readers are key.

Talk to an Expert – Stay Curious If you could ask an author anything, what would you ask them? (It's a great idea to try to find one!) Speaking with a professional can give you amazing insights into their world. Here are some ideas to get you started: "What's the most rewarding part of writing?" or "How do you overcome writer's block?" or "What advice would you give to aspiring authors?"

Bonus Activity

Explore stories by famous authors. Ask your teacher or librarian for book or movie recommendations!

Books:

Movies:

Rate This Profession

On a scale of 1 (not interested) to 10 (dream job), how well does this profession suit your personality and interests?

1 2 3 4 5 6 7 8 9 10

12. PHOTOGRAPHER

A photographer captures moments, emotions, and stories through images. Photographers use cameras and editing tools to create visual art, documenting everything from nature to people, events, or abstract concepts. They can specialize in different types of photography, such as portrait, landscape, photojournalism, or commercial photography.

Your Mission – Imagine you're a photographer!

Capture the Perfect Shot What kind of photo would you take? A breathtaking landscape, a candid moment, or a striking portrait? How would you frame the subject?

The Photographer's Tools What tools would you use—a camera, lens, tripod, or maybe drones? What's the most important equipment for capturing your perfect shot?

A Day in the Life of a Photographer Imagine you're out in the field capturing photos. Would you be shooting in a studio, traveling to an event, or exploring nature? What does your day look like?

Dream Photography Project If you could work on any photography project, what would it be? Would you document a global event, create a wildlife photo series, or explore architectural photography?

Skills for Success: What skills are important for photographers? Creativity, technical knowledge, an eye for detail, and the ability to work under pressure?

Talk to an Expert – Questions for a Photographer

If you could ask a photographer anything, what would you ask? Maybe, "What's the most memorable photo you've taken?" or "How do you stay inspired and creative?" or "What advice would you give to someone starting in photography?"

Bonus Activity

Explore photography from different genres. Ask your teacher or librarian for book or movie recommendations!

Books:

Movies:

Rate This Profession

On a scale of 1 (not interested) to 10 (dream job), how well does this profession suit your personality and interests?

1   2   3   4   5   6   7   8   9   10

13. MARINE BIOLOGIST

A marine biologist studies ocean ecosystems, marine life, and species interactions. They explore everything from plankton to whales, helping us understand the health of oceans and how to protect marine life. Marine biologists work in research, conservation, or education.

Your Mission – Imagine you're a marine biologist!

Explore the Ocean What creatures would you study—coral reefs, marine mammals, or fish?

The Research Process What research would you do—track sea turtles, study pollution impacts, or explore ecosystems?

Marine Biologist's Tools What tools would you use—diving gear, water samplers, or underwater cameras?

A Day in the Life What would your day look like—collecting samples, analyzing data, or teaching about conservation?

Dream Marine Discovery What would you discover—a new species, underwater treasures, or ways to protect endangered marine life?

Skills for Success Curiosity, research skills, knowledge of marine ecosystems, and the ability to work in tough environments are key.

Talk to an Expert – Questions for a Marine Biologist: "What's the most exciting discovery you've made?" or "What challenges do you face in ocean research?" or "What advice would you give to someone wanting to become a marine biologist?"

Bonus Activity

Explore marine biology from different genres. Ask your teacher or librarian for book or movie recommendations!

Books:

Movies:

Rate This Profession

On a scale of 1 (not interested) to 10 (dream job), how well does this profession suit your personality and interests?

1   2   3   4   5   6   7   8   9   10

14. DANCER

A dancer expresses emotions, stories, and ideas through movement, often to music. Dancers perform in various styles, such as ballet, hip-hop, contemporary, jazz, or ballroom, and work in theaters, dance companies, or as independent performers. The art of dance combines physical skill, creativity, and emotional expression.

Your Mission – Imagine you're a dancer!

Dance Style What style of dance would you perform—ballet, hip-hop, contemporary, or maybe something else?

Choreograph a Routine Imagine you're creating your own dance. What would it look like? Would it tell a story, express an emotion, or simply celebrate movement?

Dancer's Tools What tools would you need for your dance? Think about shoes, costumes, or the right space for practice. What's essential for your performances?

A Day in the Life of a Dancer Imagine you're preparing for a big performance. What does your day look like—rehearsing, stretching, or maybe working on your technique?

Dream Performance If you could perform anywhere, where would it be—on a Broadway stage, in a dance competition, or in front of a live audience at a theater?

Skills for Success

What skills are important for a dancer? Flexibility, strength, discipline, creativity, and the ability to perform under pressure?

Talk to an Expert – Questions for a Dancer

If you could talk to a professional dancer, what would you ask them? "What's the hardest part of being a dancer?" or "How do you stay motivated during tough rehearsals?" or "What advice would you give to someone who wants to become a dancer?"

Bonus Activity

Ask your teacher or librarian for books or movies about famous dancers.
Books:

Movies:

Rate This Profession

On a scale of 1 (not interested) to 10 (dream job), how well does this profession suit your personality and interests?

1 2 3 4 5 6 7 8 9 10

15. ATHLETE

An athlete is someone who competes in sports using physical skills, strength, and endurance to perform at the highest level. Athletes can participate in individual or team sports, such as soccer, basketball, track and field, swimming or tennis. They train hard, push their limits, and work toward achieving personal and professional goals.

Your Mission – Imagine you're an athlete!

Sport of Choice What sport would you compete in—soccer, basketball, swimming, or maybe something else? What makes this sport exciting for you?

Training Session Imagine you're training for a big event. What does your workout look like? Would you focus on strength, agility, endurance, or technique?

Athlete's Tools What gear would you need for your sport—shoes, uniforms, or specialized equipment?

A Day in the Life of an Athlete Imagine your daily routine as a professional athlete. Would you be training, competing, or recovering after a tough workout? What does your day look like?

Dream Achievement If you could win any major competition, what would it be—an Olympic medal, a world championship, or a professional championship in your sport?

Skills for Success What skills are important for a successful athlete? Physical strength, mental toughness, discipline, and teamwork?

Questions for an Athlete If you could talk to a professional athlete, what would you ask them? Maybe, "What's the toughest challenge you've faced in your career?" or "How do you stay focused and motivated?" or "What advice would you give to someone who wants to become an athlete?"

Bonus Activity

Learn more about the training routines of professional athletes. Ask your teacher or librarian for books or documentaries about famous athletes
Books:

Movies:

Rate This Profession
On a scale of 1 (not interested) to 10 (dream job), how well does this profession suit your personality and interests?
1 2 3 4 5 6 7 8 9 10

16. FASHION DESIGNER

A fashion designer creates clothing and accessories, blending art, style, and creativity. They work in areas like haute couture, ready-to-wear, or sustainable fashion.

Your Mission – Imagine you're a fashion designer!

Design Your Collection Imagine designing a new fashion collection. What types of clothing would you create—gowns, casual wear, or streetwear? What fabrics and colors would you choose?

Fashion Inspiration Where do you find your design inspiration? Nature, art, history, or trends? How do you turn ideas into wearable art?

Designer's Tools What tools do you need—sketchbooks, fabric swatches, sewing machines, or digital design software?

A Day in the Life of a Fashion Designer What does a busy day look like? Would you be sketching, choosing fabrics, or overseeing fittings with models?

Dream Fashion Show Where would you showcase your designs—Paris Fashion Week, Milan, or a celebrity event?

Skills for Success What skills are key for a fashion designer? Creativity, attention to detail, sewing skills, and staying ahead of trends?

Talk to an Expert – Questions for a Fashion Designer
If you could talk to a fashion designer, what would you ask? "What's your favorite part of the design process?" or "How do you stay inspired each season?" or "What advice would you give to aspiring designers?"

Bonus Activity
Explore famous fashion designers and their impact. Ask your teacher or librarian for books or documentaries about fashion.
Books:

Movies:

Rate This Profession
On a scale of 1 (not interested) to 10 (dream job), how well does this profession suit your personality and interests?
1 2 3 4 5 6 7 8 9 10

17. GAME DEVELOPER

A game developer designs, builds, and programs video games, combining creativity, coding, and problem-solving. They work in teams to create interactive experiences for players on consoles, computers, or mobile devices. Specialization includes game design, programming, animation, and sound.

Your Mission – Imagine you're a game developer!

Design Your Game What type of game would you create—adventure, puzzle, or action-packed shooter? What's the story or goal?

Character Creation Describe your game's character. What do they look like? What are their abilities and challenges?

Game Developer's Tools What tools or software would you use—coding languages, game engines, or graphics programs?

A Day in the Life What would your day look like—writing code, testing the game, or working on graphics and animation?

Dream Game Project If you could create any game, what would it be—fantasy, futuristic, or based on real-life history?

Skills for Success What skills are key—problem-solving, creativity, teamwork, and programming languages like C++ or Unity?

Talk to an Expert – Stay Curious

If you could talk to a game developer, what would you ask? Maybe, "What's the most challenging part of game development?" or "How do you stay creative when designing a game?" or "What advice would you give to aspiring game developers?"

Bonus Activity

Explore game development by playing different types of games. Ask your teacher or librarian for books or articles on game creation.

Books:

Movies:

Rate This Profession

On a scale of 1 (not interested) to 10 (dream job), how well does this profession suit your personality and interests?

1 2 3 4 5 6 7 8 9 10

18. CONSTRUCTION WORKER

A construction worker builds and maintains structures like buildings, roads, and bridges. They use tools and machinery to bring designs to life, specializing in carpentry, masonry, plumbing, or electrical work.

Your Mission – Imagine you're a construction worker!
Build Your Project Imagine you're building a structure. What would it be—residential, commercial, or infrastructure? What materials would you use?
The Tools of the Trade What tools are essential for your work—hammer, cement mixer, or scaffolding?
A Day in the Life What would your day be like on a construction site? Would you be measuring, lifting, or working with your team?
Dream Construction Project If you could work on any project, what would it be—a skyscraper, a bridge, or a green building?
Skills for Success What skills are important in construction—precision, physical stamina, problem-solving, and teamwork?
Talk to an Expert – Questions for a Construction Worker
If you could ask a construction worker anything, what would you ask? "What's the most challenging part of construction?" or "How do you stay safe on-site?" or "What advice would you give to someone starting in construction?"

Bonus Activity
Explore stories of famous construction projects. Ask your teacher or librarian for recommendations.
Books:

Movies:

Rate This Profession
On a scale of 1 (not interested) to 10 (dream job), how well does this profession suit your personality and interests?
1 2 3 4 5 6 7 8 9 10

19. ZOOLOGIST

A zoologist studies animals, their behavior, genetics, physiology, and interactions with ecosystems. They explore everything from tiny insects to large mammals, helping us understand wildlife conservation, animal behavior, and environmental changes. Zoologists work in research, conservation, education, or zoos.

Your Mission – Imagine you're a zoologist!

Explore Animal Kingdoms What animals would you focus on—endangered species, primates, or marine life?

Research Focus What research would you conduct—tracking animal behavior, studying genetics, or exploring habitat loss?

Zoologist's Tools What tools would you use—tracking devices, microscopes, or field observation tools?

A Day in the Life What would your day look like—collecting data, studying animal habitats, or educating the public on conservation?

Dream Discovery If you could make any discovery, what would it be—finding a new species, uncovering animal behavior patterns, or contributing to wildlife conservation?

Skills for Success Strong observation skills, knowledge of animal behavior, research expertise, and an understanding of ecosystems are essential.

Talk to an Expert – Stay Curious

If you could ask a zoologist anything, what would you ask? You can try: "What's the most exciting discovery you've made in your zoology career?" or "How do you overcome challenges in wildlife conservation?" or "What advice would you give to someone wanting to become a zoologist?"

Bonus Activity

Explore stories of famous construction projects. Ask your teacher or librarian for recommendations.

Books:

Movies:

Rate This Profession

On a scale of 1 (not interested) to 10 (dream job), how well does this profession suit your personality and interests?

1   2   3   4   5   6   7   8   9   10

20. PILOT

A pilot operates aircraft to safely transport passengers or cargo. They are trained in navigation, flight planning, and handling various aircraft systems, working for airlines, cargo companies, or private charters.

Your Mission – Imagine you're a pilot!

Flight Plan What's your route and what do you need to consider—weather, fuel, or air traffic control?

Aircraft Control How do you navigate the plane, and what instruments do you rely on?

Pilot's Tools What tools do pilots use—navigation systems, flight plans, or communication equipment?

A Day in the Life What does a typical day look like for you? Flying, pre-flight checks, or talking with air traffic control?

Dream Destination Where would you love to fly? A popular spot, an exotic place, or a remote area?

Skills for Success What skills are important for pilots—quick thinking, communication, and technical knowledge?

Talk to an Expert – Questions for a Pilot

What would you ask a pilot? Maybe, "What's the hardest part of flying?" or "How do you manage stressful situations?" or "What advice would you give to future pilots?"

Bonus Activity

Learn more about aviation. Ask your teacher or librarian for books or documentaries.

Books:

Movies:

Rate This Profession
On a scale of 1 (not interested) to 10 (dream job), how well does this profession suit your personality and interests?
1   2   3   4   5   6   7   8   9   10

21. NURSE

A nurse provides care to patients, assisting doctors and supporting patients through treatments and recovery. Nurses work in hospitals, clinics, and other healthcare settings, focusing on health monitoring, patient education, and emotional support.

Your Mission – Imagine you're a nurse!

Patient Care What type of patients would you care for—children, the elderly, or those in critical condition?

Medical Tools What tools would you use—stethoscopes, thermometers, or medical charts?

A Day in the Life What does a typical shift look like? Would you be assisting with procedures, monitoring vital signs, or comforting patients?

Dream Hospital Role If you could work in any department, which one would it be? Emergency, pediatrics, or intensive care?

Skills for Success What skills are important for a nurse—compassion, attention to detail, or the ability to stay calm under pressure?

Talk to an Expert – Questions for a Nurse

What would you ask a nurse? Maybe, "What's the most rewarding part of being a nurse?" or "How do you handle the emotional challenges?" or "What advice would you give to someone wanting to become a nurse?"

Bonus Activity

Explore nursing stories or watch medical dramas. Ask your teacher or librarian for recommendations.

Books:

Movies:

Rate This Profession

On a scale of 1 (not interested) to 10 (dream job), how well does this profession suit your personality and interests?

1   2   3   4   5   6   7   8   9   10

22. LIBRARIAN

A librarian helps people find information, manages library resources, and promotes reading and learning. They work in libraries, schools, and other educational settings, organizing books, digital resources, and assisting with research.

Your Mission – Imagine you're a librarian!

Organize the Library What kind of system would you use to organize books—alphabetical, by genre, or by theme?

Reading Recommendations What book would you recommend to someone who loves adventure?

Librarian's Tools What tools would you use—cataloging systems, computers, or library apps?

A Day in the Life of a Librarian What would your day look like? Would you be helping patrons find books, planning events, or managing the library's collection?

Dream Library Project If you could create a library space, what would it include? Quiet study areas, a reading nook, or community programs?

Skills for Success What skills are important for a librarian—organization, communication, and a love for reading and learning?

Talk to an Expert – Speaking with a professional can give you amazing insights into their world. Here are a few questions to spark your imagination: "What's the most rewarding part of being a librarian?" or "How do you help people who aren't sure what book to read?" or "What advice would you give to someone who wants to become a librarian?"

Bonus Activity
Explore famous libraries around the world, or learn about history of libraries. Ask your teacher or librarian for recommendations.
Books:

Movies:

Rate This Profession
On a scale of 1 (not interested) to 10 (dream job), how well does this profession suit your personality and interests?
1 2 3 4 5 6 7 8 9 10

23. ARCHITECT

An architect designs buildings and structures, blending creativity, functionality, and safety. They work on everything from homes and schools to skyscrapers and bridges, ensuring their designs meet the needs of people and the environment.

Your Mission – Imagine you're an architect!

Design Your Dream Building What kind of building would you design—a modern home, a skyscraper, or a cultural center? What features would it have?

Architecture Inspiration Where do you get your ideas—nature, other cultures, or famous landmarks?

Architect's Tools What tools would you use to design—blueprints, software like AutoCAD, or models?

A Day in the Life of an Architect What would your day look like—sketching new designs, meeting clients, or reviewing construction plans?

Dream Architecture Project If you could design any project, what would it be—a sustainable city, a futuristic museum, or a landmark?

Skills for Success What skills are important to be a successful architect—creativity, problem-solving, attention to detail, and knowledge of construction?

Talk to an Expert, Ask Questions Here are a few questions to spark your imagination: "What's the most challenging part of designing a building?" or "How do you ensure your designs are both beautiful and practical?" or "What advice would you give to someone who wants to become an architect?"

Bonus Activity

Explore famous buildings and the architects behind them. Ask your teacher or librarian for book or movie recommendations.

Books:

Movies:

Rate This Profession

On a scale of 1 (not interested) to 10 (dream job), how well does this profession suit your personality and interests?

1 2 3 4 5 6 7 8 9 10

24. SOCIAL WORKER

A social worker helps individuals and communities navigate challenges like mental health issues, family problems, or poverty. They offer support, resources, and guidance to improve well-being in settings like schools, hospitals, or government agencies.

Your Mission – Imagine you're a social worker!

Helping a Client How would you assist someone facing a tough situation—through counseling, resources, or connecting them to other services?

Support Network How would you build a support system for someone—family, friends, or community services?

Social Worker's Tools What tools would you use—communication skills, therapy techniques, or databases?

A Day in the Life What would a typical day involve—meeting clients, attending meetings, or planning programs?

Dream Project If you could work on any issue—mental health, homelessness, or children's education—what would it be?

Skills for Success What skills are essential for a social worker—empathy, communication, and problem-solving?

Talk to an Expert – Questions for a Social Worker:
"What's the most rewarding part of your job?" or "How do you manage emotional challenges?" or "What advice would you give to someone entering this field?"

Bonus Activity

Explore social work in different settings. Ask your teacher or librarian for book or movie recommendations.

Books:

Movies:

Rate This Profession
On a scale of 1 (not interested) to 10 (dream job), how well does this profession suit your personality and interests?
1 2 3 4 5 6 7 8 9 10

25. ASTRONOMER

Astronomers study celestial objects like stars, planets, and galaxies. They use telescopes and data analysis to understand the origins of the universe, structure, and evolution. Astronomers work in observatories, research institutions, or universities.

Your Mission – Imagine you're an astronomer!

Explore the Universe What celestial body would you study—planets, stars, or black holes? What would you want to learn about it?

Astronomical Discovery Imagine you make a new discovery. What is it—an unknown planet, a new galaxy, or a new star formation?

Astronomer's Tools What tools would you need—telescopes, satellites, or computer software?

A Day on the Job What does your day look like—observing the sky, analyzing data, or writing research papers?

Dream Project If you could research anything in space—extraterrestrial life, dark matter, or the formation of the universe—what would it be?

Skills for Success What skills are important for an astronomer—mathematics, problem-solving, and critical thinking?

Talk to an Expert – Questions for an Astronomer

What would you ask an astronomer? "What's the most exciting discovery you've made?" or "How do you gather data on distant objects?" or "What advice would you give to someone wanting to become an astronomer?"

Bonus Activity

Explore space and astronomy through documentaries and books. Ask your teacher or librarian for recommendations.

Books:

Movies:

Rate This Profession

On a scale of 1 (not interested) to 10 (dream job), how well does this profession suit your personality and interests?

1 2 3 4 5 6 7 8 9 10

26. GRAPHIC DESIGNER

A graphic designer creates visual content for print, digital media, advertising, and more. They use design software and creativity to communicate messages, tell stories, and captivate audiences through layouts, logos, and images.

Your Mission – Imagine you're a graphic designer!

Design Your Project Imagine you're designing a logo or an advertisement. What colors, fonts, and images would you use to make it stand out?

Creative Process Where do you find your inspiration—nature, art, or everyday life? How do you turn ideas into visuals?

Designer's Tools What tools would you use—Adobe Illustrator, Photoshop, or a drawing tablet?

A Day in the Life What does your day look like—brainstorming ideas, creating drafts, or collaborating with clients?

Dream Project If you could design anything, what would it be—a brand identity, a magazine cover, or an app interface?

Skills for Success What skills are important for a graphic designer—creativity, attention to detail, and proficiency in design software?

Talk to an Expert – Stay Curious

What would you ask a graphic designer? Maybe, "What's your favorite type of design project?" or "How do you handle creative blocks?" or "What advice would you give to someone wanting to become a graphic designer?"

Bonus Activity

Explore the work of famous graphic designers. Ask your teacher or librarian for books or documentaries about design.

Books:

Movies:

Rate This Profession

On a scale of 1 (not interested) to 10 (dream job), how well does this profession suit your personality and interests?

1 2 3 4 5 6 7 8 9 10

27. POLICE OFFICER

A police officer maintains law and order, protects citizens, and enforces laws. They investigate crimes, respond to emergencies, and ensure public safety.

Your Mission – Imagine you're a police officer!

Law Enforcement Tools What tools do you need—a badge, handcuffs, radio, or patrol car?

Handling Emergencies Imagine responding to an emergency. What's your first step—assess the scene, help, or gather evidence?

A Day in the Life What would a typical day look like—patrolling, investigating, or solving a case?

Dream Assignment What case or investigation would you want to work on—robbery, missing person, or cybercrime?

Community Interaction How would you build trust and prevent crime in the community?

Skills for Success What skills are important for a police officer—communication, problem-solving, fitness, and staying calm under pressure?

Talk to an Expert – Ask Questions to a Police Officer

Here are a few questions to spark your imagination: "What's the toughest part of your job?" or "How do you manage stress?" or "What advice would you give someone who wants to join law enforcement?"

Bonus Activity

Explore stories about police officers. Ask for recommendations.
Books:

Movies:

Rate This Profession

On a scale of 1 (not interested) to 10 (dream job), how well does this profession suit your personality and interests?

1 2 3 4 5 6 7 8 9 10

28. ENVIRONMENTAL SCIENTIST

An environmental scientist studies the environment and works to protect it. They research issues like pollution, climate change, and conservation to develop solutions for a healthier planet.

Your Mission – Imagine you're an environmental scientist!

Research Project What environmental issue would you focus on—air pollution, deforestation, or wildlife conservation?

Data Collection What tools would you use—satellite images, water samples, or field research?

A Day in the Life What's your day like—collecting samples, analyzing data, or presenting findings?

Dream Environmental Solution What problem would you solve—restoring ecosystems, reducing waste, or combating climate change?

Collaboration How would you work with communities or governments to make an impact?

Skills for Success What skills are essential—critical thinking, research, data analysis, and environmental awareness?

Talk to an Expert – Stay Curious

What would you ask an environmental scientist? Try this: What's the biggest challenge today?" or "How do you stay motivated?" or "What advice would you give someone starting in this field?"

Bonus Activity

Explore environmental topics and solutions. Ask for book or documentary recommendations.

Books:

Movies:

Rate This Profession

On a scale of 1 (not interested) to 10 (dream job), how well does this profession suit your personality and interests?

1 2 3 4 5 6 7 8 9 10

29. HAIR STYLIST

A hair stylist is a professional who cuts, colors, and styles hair to help people look and feel their best. They work in salons, spas, or even on set for photo shoots and fashion shows, creating trendy personalized looks for their clients.

Your Mission – Imagine you're a hair stylist!

Design Your Look Imagine you're creating a new hairstyle. What type of cut or color would you choose—bold, edgy, or classic?

Styling Tools What tools would you use to style hair—scissors, blow dryers, straighteners, or hair color?

A Day in the Life What does your day look like—cutting hair, consulting with clients, or coloring and styling?

Dream Client If you could style anyone's hair, who would it be—perhaps a celebrity or someone with a unique hair challenge?

Trendy Styles How do you stay up-to-date with the latest hair trends and techniques?

Skills for Success What skills are important to be a successful stylist—creativity, attention to detail, technical skills, and good communication?

Talk to an Expert – Questions for a Hair Stylist

What would you ask a professional hair stylist? Maybe, What's your favorite hairstyle to create?" or "How do you handle challenging hair types or requests?" or "What advice would you give to someone becoming a hair stylist?"

Bonus Activity

Explore hairstyling tutorials or learn about famous stylists and their work.
Books:

Movies:

Rate This Profession

On a scale of 1 (not interested) to 10 (dream job), how well does this profession suit your personality and interests?

1   2   3   4   5   6   7   8   9   10

30. ELECTRICIAN

An electrician installs, maintains, and repairs electrical systems in homes, buildings, and other structures. They work with wiring, circuit breakers, and electrical equipment to ensure everything operates safely and efficiently.

Your Mission – Imagine you're an electrician!

Wiring a House Imagine you're wiring a house. What steps would you take to make sure the system is safe and reliable?

Tools of the Trade What tools would you use—wire cutters, drills, voltmeters, or power testers?

A Day in the Life What's your day like—installing new systems, troubleshooting problems, or testing equipment?

Dream Project If you could work on any electrical project, what would it be—designing a sustainable energy system, building smart homes, or setting up an electrical grid?

Safety First How would you ensure safety on the job?

Skills for Success What skills are important—attention to detail, problem-solving, and knowledge of electrical systems and safety?

Talk to an Expert – Questions for an Electrician

What would you ask an electrician? Try this: "What's the most challenging part of your job?" or "How do you stay up to date with new technology?" or "What advice would you give to someone wanting to become an electrician?"

Bonus Activity

Explore how electricity powers homes and industries. Ask for book or documentary recommendations.

Books:

Movies:

Rate This Profession

On a scale of 1 (not interested) to 10 (dream job), how well does this profession suit your personality and interests?

1   2   3   4   5   6   7   8   9   10

31. MATHEMATICIAN

A mathematician uses numbers, formulas, and logic to solve problems and understand patterns. They work in various fields, from pure mathematics to applied areas like engineering, finance, or technology, making complex ideas easier to understand and apply.

Your Mission – Imagine you're a mathematician!

Solving a Problem Imagine you're solving a complex equation. How would you approach it—using algebra, calculus, or logic?

Mathematical Tools What tools would you use—calculators, computers, or mathematical software?

A Day in the Life What's your day like—working on theories, collaborating with other scientists, or presenting your findings?

Dream Mathematical Challenge If you could tackle any mathematical problem, what would it be—discovering new theories, solving global issues, or advancing technology?

Collaboration How would you work with other experts, such as scientists or engineers to apply mathematical solutions in real-world problems?

Skills for Success What skills are important—critical thinking, problem-solving, and in-depth knowledge of mathematics?

Talk to an Expert – Ask questions to a mathematician.

Here are a few questions to spark your imagination: "What's the most exciting part of working in mathematics?" or "How do you stay motivated while tackling difficult problems?" or "What advice would you give to someone who wants to become a mathematician?"

Bonus Activity

Explore famous mathematicians and their contributions. Ask for book or documentary recommendations.

Books:

Movies:

Rate This Profession

On a scale of 1 (not interested) to 10 (dream job), how well does this profession suit your personality and interests?

1 2 3 4 5 6 7 8 9 10

32. HISTORIAN

A historian studies the past to understand how events, people, and societies have shaped the world. They analyze documents, artifacts, and records to uncover stories, patterns, and lessons from history, helping us learn from the past to inform the future.

>**Your Mission** – Imagine you're a historian!
>
>**Research a Topic** Imagine you're researching a historical event. What would you focus on—ancient civilizations, World War II, or the history of a specific culture?
>
>**Historical Tools** What tools would you use—books, archives, interviews, or digital databases?
>
>**A Day in the Life** What does your day look like—conducting research, visiting museums, or writing papers and articles?
>
>**Dream Historical Discovery** If you could uncover any historical mystery, what would it be—lost civilizations, ancient texts, or hidden artifacts?
>
>**Collaboration** How would you work with other experts, such as archaeologists or museum curators to preserve history?
>
>**Skills for Success** What skills are important—research, critical thinking, writing, and attention to detail?
>
>**Talk to an Expert – Stay Curious** What would you ask a historian? "What's the most interesting historical event you've studied?" or "How do you verify the accuracy of historical records?" or "What advice would you give to someone who wants to become a historian?"

Bonus Activity
Explore historical topics or time periods. Ask for book or documentary recommendations.
Books:

Movies:

>**Rate This Profession**
>On a scale of 1 (not interested) to 10 (dream job), how well does this profession suit your personality and interests?
>1   2   3   4   5   6   7   8   9   10

33. INTERIOR DESIGNER

An interior designer creates beautiful functional spaces by selecting furniture, colors, lighting, and décor. They work in homes, offices, and public spaces to enhance the aesthetics and usability of an area, ensuring it meets the client's needs and style.

Your Mission – Imagine you're an interior designer!

Design a Room Imagine you're designing a living room or office. What furniture, colors, and layouts would you choose?

Design Inspiration Where do you get your inspiration—nature, art, fashion, or architectural styles?

Designer's Tools What tools would you use—sketches, computer design software, or material samples?

A Day in the Life What does your day look like—consulting clients, shopping for furniture, or overseeing installations?

Dream Design Project If you could design any space, what would it be—a luxury hotel, modern office, or eco-friendly home?

Skills for Success What skills are important—creativity, attention to detail, problem-solving, and knowledge of design principles?

Talk to an Expert – Stay Curious What would you ask an interior designer? Try this: "How do you create a design that fits the client's needs?" or "What's your favorite style of design?" or "What advice would you give to someone pursuing interior design?"

Bonus Activity

Explore different design styles. Ask for book or magazine recommendations.
Books:

Movies:

Rate This Profession
On a scale of 1 (not interested) to 10 (dream job), how well does this profession suit your personality and interests?

1 2 3 4 5 6 7 8 9 10

34. SOUND ENGINEER

A sound engineer works with audio equipment to capture, manipulate, and enhance sound for music, movies, live events, or broadcasts. They mix, record, and edit sound to create the perfect audio experience, ensuring everything sounds clear and balanced.

>**Your Mission** – Imagine you're a sound engineer!
>
>**Design the Sound** Imagine you're designing sound for a music track or film scene. What equipment and techniques would you use to create the right mood or atmosphere?
>
>**Sound Equipment** What tools would you use—microphones, mixers, software, or headphones?
>
>**A Day in the Life** What does your day look like—recording sound, mixing audio, or working on post-production?
>
>**Dream Sound Project** If you could work on any audio project, what would it be—recording a live concert, editing movie sound effects, or mixing an album?
>
>**Skills for Success** What skills are important—technical knowledge of audio equipment, creativity, attention to detail, and problem-solving?
>
>**Talk to an Expert** – What would you ask a sound engineer? "What's the most challenging part of sound engineering?" or "How do you stay creative while working with audio?" or "What advice would you give to someone entering this field?"

Bonus Activity

Explore different aspects of sound design. Ask for book or movie recommendations about sound engineering.

Books:

Movies: **Rate This Profession**

On a scale of 1 (not interested) to 10 (dream job), how well does this profession suit your personality and interests?

1 2 3 4 5 6 7 8 9 10

35. NUTRITIONIST

A nutritionist helps people make healthy food choices to improve their overall well-being. They study the relationship between food and health, providing advice on diets, meal plans, and nutrition for various health conditions.

Your Mission – Imagine you're a nutritionist!

Design a Meal Plan Imagine you're creating a meal plan for a friend. Would it focus on weight loss, boosting energy, or managing a health condition like diabetes?

Nutrition Tools What tools would you use—food journals, nutritional software, or recipes?

A Day in the Life What does your day look like—counseling clients, researching nutrition trends, or planning meals?

Dream Client If you could work with anyone, who would it be—an athlete, a child with dietary needs, or someone managing a chronic illness?

Skills for Success What skills are essential—understanding nutrition science, communication, empathy, and problem-solving?

Talk to an Expert – What would you ask a nutritionist? "What's the most common nutrition myth you hear?" or "How do you help clients stay motivated to eat healthier?" or "What advice would you give to someone pursuing a career in nutrition?"

Bonus Activity

Explore nutrition and healthy eating. Ask for recommendations on books or documentaries.

Books:

Movies:

Rate This Profession
On a scale of 1 (not interested) to 10 (dream job),
how well does this profession suit your personality and interests?
1   2   3   4   5   6   7   8   9   10

36. PUBLIC SPEAKER

A public speaker communicates ideas, inspires, and educates people on various topics. They work in diverse fields such as business, motivation, education, and advocacy. Public speakers can speak at events, conferences, or in front of large crowds to share knowledge and influence others.

Your Mission – Imagine you're a public speaker!

Create Your Speech Imagine you're preparing a speech. What topic would you choose—motivation, leadership, or social change? How would you make it engaging for your audience?

Public Speaking Tools What tools would you need—a microphone, presentation slides, or notes?

A Day in the Life What does your day look like—practicing your speech, meeting event organizers, or addressing an audience?

Dream Speaking Engagement If you could speak at any event, where would it be—an international conference, a TED talk, or a motivational seminar?

Skills for Success What skills are important—confidence, clear communication, storytelling, and the ability to connect with your audience?

Talk to an Expert – What would you ask a professional speaker? Maybe, "How do you deal with stage fright?" or "What's the most rewarding part of speaking to an audience?" or "What advice would you give to someone starting as a public speaker?"

Bonus Activity
Watch speeches by famous public speakers. Ask for recommendations on books or videos about effective speaking.
Books:

Movies:

Rate This Profession
On a scale of 1 (not interested) to 10 (dream job),
how well does this profession suit your personality and interests?
1   2   3   4   5   6   7   8   9   10

37. ACCOUNTANT

An accountant manages financial records, prepares reports, and ensures that businesses or individuals comply with financial regulations. They work with budgets, taxes, and audits, helping to keep finances organized and transparent.

Your Mission – Imagine you're an accountant!

Manage a Budget Imagine you're creating a budget for a company. How would you allocate funds for different departments—marketing, operations, and salaries?

Financial Reports What kind of reports would you prepare—profit and loss statements, balance sheets, or tax returns ((useful tools to track money—you'll learn about them one day!)

Accountant's Tools What tools or software would you use to keep financial records accurate—spreadsheets, accounting software, or calculators?

A Day in the Life What does your day look like—analyzing financial data, meeting clients, or preparing tax filings?

Dream Accounting Project If you could work on any accounting project, what would it be—helping a business reduce taxes, conducting an audit, or managing investments?

Skills for Success What skills are essential—attention to detail, strong math abilities, organization, and knowledge of tax laws and financial regulations?

Talk to an Expert – Accountant Q&A What would you ask a professional accountant? "How do you keep track of all the financial data?" or "What's the most challenging part of working with finances?" or "What advice would you give to someone who wants to become an accountant?"

Bonus Activity

Explore resources about financial literacy. Ask for recommendations on books or articles about managing money and budgeting.
Books:

Websites:

Movies: Rate This Profession
On a scale of 1 (not interested) to 10 (dream job), how well does this profession suit your personality and interests?
1   2   3   4   5   6   7   8   9   10

38. COACH

A coach helps athletes improve their skills, develop strategies, and motivates individuals or teams to achieve their goals. Coaches work in sports, fitness, or personal development, guiding others through training, performance, and competitions.

Your Mission – Imagine you're a coach!

Create a Training Plan Imagine you're designing a training plan for your team. What exercises, drills, and techniques would you focus on to improve their performance?

Motivation Techniques How would you motivate your athletes during tough times? Would you give pep talks, set achievable goals, or offer rewards?

Coach's Tools What tools would you use to train athletes—whistles, video analysis, training equipment, or fitness apps?

A Day in the Life What would your day look like—leading a practice session, analyzing performance, or meeting with athletes?

Dream Coaching Opportunity If you could coach any team or individual, who would it be—your favorite athletic team, an Olympic athlete, or a community team?

Skills for Success What skills are important—leadership, communication, strategic thinking, knowledge of sports, or fitness?

Talk to an Expert - What would you ask a professional coach? Maybe, "What's the hardest part of coaching?" or "How do you keep your athletes motivated?" or "What advice would you give to someone who wants to become a coach?"

Bonus Activity
Explore stories of famous coaches and their impact on sports. Ask for book or documentary recommendations.
Books:

Movies:

Rate This Profession
On a scale of 1 (not interested) to 10 (dream job), how well does this profession suit your personality and interests?
1   2   3   4   5   6   7   8   9   10

39. MOVIE DIRECTOR

A movie director is responsible for bringing a story to life on screen. They work closely with actors, writers, and the production team to create a vision for the film, making decisions on everything from casting to camera angles, lighting, and sound.

Your Mission – Imagine you're a movie director!

Create Your Film Imagine you're directing a new movie. What genre would it be—action, drama, comedy, or thriller? What's the plot, and who are the key characters?

Directing Actors How would you guide your actors to bring their characters to life? Would you focus on emotions, timing, or improvisation?

Director's Tools What tools would you use—camera equipment, storyboards, editing software, or maybe a script to guide the team?

A Day in the Life What would your day look like on set—directing scenes, collaborating with the crew, or reviewing takes?

Dream Film Project If you could direct any film, what would it be? Would you remake a classic, tell a personal story, or create an entirely new world?

Skills for Success What skills are essential—creativity, leadership, communication, problem-solving, and a strong understanding of film production?

Talk to an Expert – Stay Curious What would you ask a professional director? Try this: "What's the most challenging part of directing a film?" or "How do you balance creativity with practical constraints on set?" or "What advice would you give to someone wanting to become a movie director?"

Bonus Activity

Explore the work of famous directors and their impact on cinema. Ask for recommendations on films or documentaries about filmmaking.

Books:

Movies:

Rate This Profession
On a scale of 1 (not interested) to 10 (dream job), how well does this profession suit your personality and interests?
1   2   3   4   5   6   7   8   9   10

40. WEB DEVELOPER

A web developer builds and maintains websites and applications. They write code, design user interfaces, and ensure that all sites work on all devices. Developers can focus on front-end (what users see) or back-end (functionality) development.

Your Mission – Imagine you're a web developer!

Design Your Website What's your site's purpose—an online store, blog, or portfolio? What design elements would you choose—colors, layout, and navigation?

Coding Challenge What programming languages would you use—HTML, CSS, JavaScript, or something else? *(Don't worry if you don't know coding—you can learn easily!)*

Developer's Tools What tools or software would you use—text editors, coding frameworks, or version control tools?

A Day in the Life What would your day look like—coding, fixing bugs, collaborating with clients, or testing sites?

Dream Web Project If you could create any site or app, what would it be? A social network, educational platform, or something else?

Skills for Success What skills are important for success—problem-solving, coding, attention to detail, and teamwork?

Talk to an Expert – Stay Curious What would you ask a web developer? "What's the most exciting part of building a website?" or "How do you stay current with new technologies?" or "What advice would you give someone learning web development?"

Bonus Activity

Explore web development resources and learn coding basics. Ask for recommendations on books or tutorials.

Books:

Websites:

Rate This Profession
On a scale of 1 (not interested) to 10 (dream job), how well does this profession suit your personality and interests?

1   2   3   4   5   6   7   8   9   10

41. PALEONTOLOGIST

A paleontologist studies fossils to understand the history of life on Earth. They research ancient organisms, including plants, animals, and microbes, to learn about evolution, climate change, and ecosystems from the past.

Your Mission – Imagine you're a paleontologist!

Research Project What type of fossils would you study—dinosaurs, ancient plants, or marine life?

Field Work Where would you go to dig for fossils—deserts, mountains, or forests? What tools would you use?

A Day in the Life What would your day look like—excavating fossils, analyzing data, or reconstructing ancient creatures?

Dream Discovery If you could discover any fossil, what would it be—a new dinosaur species, an ancient plant, or something else?

Collaboration How would you work with other scientists to share findings and expand knowledge?

Skills for Success What skills are important—attention to detail, patience, research, and a strong understanding of biology and geology?

Talk to an Expert What would you ask a paleontologist? "What's your favorite discovery?" or "What's the most challenging part of paleontology?" or "What advice would you give to someone pursuing this field?"

Bonus Activity

Explore paleontology by reading books or watching documentaries about fossils and ancient life.

Books:

Movies:

Rate This Profession

On a scale of 1 (not interested) to 10 (dream job), how well does this profession suit your personality and interests?

1 2 3 4 5 6 7 8 9 10

42. SPORTS COMMENTATOR

A sports commentator provides live commentary and analysis during sports events. They describe the action, explain the rules, and provide insights into players, teams, and strategies to engage and inform the audience.

Your Mission – Imagine you're a sports commentator!

Favorite Sport Which sport would you commentate on—soccer, basketball, tennis, or something else? What makes it exciting to watch?

Commentary Style How would you describe action on the field? Would you focus on fast-paced moments, player stats, or the overall atmosphere?

Tools of the Trade What equipment would you use—microphones, headsets, or live scoreboards? What's essential for delivering great commentary?

A Day in the Life What would your day look like—preparing for a game, analyzing statistics, or providing live commentary?

Dream Event If you could commentate on any event, what would it be—the Super Bowl, World Cup, or the Olympics?

Skills for Success What skills are important—quick thinking, communication, knowledge of the game, and an engaging personality?

Talk to an Expert What would you ask a sports commentator? "How do you stay calm during intense moments?" or "What's your favorite part of commentating a game?" or "What advice would you give to someone aspiring to be a sports commentator?"

Bonus Activity
Watch a sports event and try your hand at commentary. Ask your teacher or librarian for books or articles on sports journalism.

Books:

Movies:

Rate This Profession
On a scale of 1 (not interested) to 10 (dream job), how well does this profession suit your personality and interests?
1 2 3 4 5 6 7 8 9 10

43. SCULPTOR

A sculptor creates three-dimensional art by shaping materials like clay, wood, metal, or stone. They design and carve sculptures that represent anything from abstract ideas to realistic figures. Sculptors work in studios, galleries, or outdoor spaces, bringing their creative visions to life.

Your Mission – Imagine you're a sculptor!

Design Your Sculpture Imagine you're designing a sculpture. What shape or figure would you create—something abstract, a human figure, or a nature-inspired piece?

Materials What materials would you use for your sculpture? Would you choose marble, bronze, wood, or maybe recycled materials?

Tools of the Trade What tools would you need to shape your sculpture—chisels, hammers, welding equipment, or 3D design software?

A Day in the Life What would your day be like as a sculptor—designing sketches, shaping materials, or refining details?

Dream Sculpture If you could create any sculpture, what would it be—a large public monument, a delicate figure, or a sculpture inspired by nature?

Skills for Success What skills are important for a sculptor—creativity, attention to detail, technical skills with materials, and patience?

Talk to an Expert What would you ask a professional sculptor? "What's the most challenging part of creating a sculpture?" or "How do you decide which materials to use?" or "What advice would you give to someone wanting to become a sculptor?"

Bonus Activity
Explore famous sculptures and artists. Ask your teacher or librarian for book recommendations or documentaries.
Books:

Movies:

Rate This Profession
On a scale of 1 (not interested) to 10 (dream job), how well does this profession suit your personality and interests?
1 2 3 4 5 6 7 8 9 10

44. METEOROLOGIST

A meteorologist studies the weather and atmospheric conditions to understand and predict weather patterns. They analyze data from satellites, radars, and weather stations to forecast conditions like rain, snow, or storms, helping people plan and stay safe.

Your Mission – Imagine you're a meteorologist!

Forecast Your Day Imagine you're forecasting the weather for tomorrow. What would you prefer to forecast — sunny, rainy, or stormy?

Tools of the Trade What tools do you use to gather weather data—satellites, radar, weather balloons, or computer models?

A Day in the Life What would your day look like—analyzing data, preparing weather reports, or broadcasting forecasts on TV?

Extreme Weather If you could focus on one extreme weather event—hurricanes, tornadoes, or blizzards—what would it be and why?

Dream Project If you could solve any weather-related problem, what would it be—predicting storms more accurately or understanding climate change better?

Skills for Success What skills are important for a meteorologist—attention to detail, problem-solving, knowledge of science, and data analysis?

Talk to an Expert What would you ask a meteorologist? "What's the most interesting weather pattern you've studied?" or "How do you predict weather during extreme conditions?" or "What advice would you give to someone who wants to become a meteorologist?"

Bonus Activity

Learn more about weather patterns and climate science. Ask your teacher or librarian for books or documentaries on meteorology.

Books:

Movies:

Rate This Profession

On a scale of 1 (not interested) to 10 (dream job), how well does this profession suit your personality and interests?

1 2 3 4 5 6 7 8 9 10

45. ANIMAL TRAINER

An animal trainer works with animals to teach specific behaviors or skills. They use positive reinforcement, patience, and consistency to train pets, working animals, or even wild animals in various settings like zoos, circuses, or movie sets.

Your Mission – Imagine you're an animal trainer!

Training Your Animal What animal would you train—a dog, horse, dolphin or bird? What would you teach it—sit, fetch, or maybe a special trick?

Training Methods What techniques would you use—treats, toys, or clickers to reward good behavior?

A Day in the Life Would your day involve training sessions, caring for animals, or working with a team?

Trainer Challenges What challenges might you face—stubborn animals, staying patient, or working outdoors?

Skills for Success What skills do animal trainers need—patience, understanding animal behavior, communication, and physical fitness?

Talk to an Expert What would you ask a professional animal trainer? "What's the hardest animal you've had to train?" or "How do you build trust with animals?" or "What advice would you give to someone starting out in animal training?"

Bonus Activity

Explore different types of animal training. Ask your teacher or librarian for books or videos on animal behavior or famous trainers.

Books:

Movies:

Rate This Profession

On a scale of 1 (not interested) to 10 (dream job), how well does this profession suit your personality and interests?

1 2 3 4 5 6 7 8 9 10

46. TRAVEL BLOGGER

A travel blogger explores different destinations, sharing their experiences, tips, and recommendations through blog posts, photos, and videos. They capture the essence of various places, cultures, and adventures, providing readers with insights and inspiration for their own travels.

Your Mission – Imagine you're a travel blogger!

Plan Your Next Adventure Imagine you're planning a trip. Where would you go—an exotic beach, a bustling city, or a peaceful mountain retreat? What's your travel theme—food, culture, or adventure?

Capturing the Moment What tools would you use to document your journey? Would you take photos, shoot videos, or keep a travel journal?

A Day in the Life What does your day look like—exploring a new city, writing blog posts, or editing videos?

Dream Travel Destination If you could visit any place in the world, where would it be, and what would you write about it?

Challenges of Blogging What challenges do you think you'd face as a travel blogger—finding time to travel, capturing the right content, or keeping your readers engaged?

Skills for Success What skills are important for a successful travel blogger—writing, photography, social media management, or an adventurous spirit?

Talk to an Expert – Stay Curious "What's your favorite destination, and why?" or "How do you stay motivated to travel and write consistently?" or "What advice would you give to someone who wants to start a travel blog?"

Bonus Activity

Explore popular travel blogs and get inspired. Ask your teacher or librarian for recommendations on travel writing books or websites.

Books:

Websites:

Rate This Profession

On a scale of 1 (not interested) to 10 (dream job), how well does this profession suit your personality and interests?

1 2 3 4 5 6 7 8 9 10

47. TOY DESIGNER

A toy designer creates fun, safe, imaginative toys for children. They blend creativity with functionality to design toys that are engaging, educational, and entertaining. Toy designers often work with materials, safety standards, and trends to develop toys that spark joy and learning.

Your Mission – Imagine you're a toy designer!

Design Your Toy Imagine you're creating a new toy. What kind of toy would it be—interactive, educational, or just for fun? What materials and colors would you use?

Toy Features What features would your toy have? Would it make sounds, move, or teach something new?

A Day in the Life What does your day look like—sketching new designs, testing prototypes, or researching the latest trends in toys?

Dream Toy Collection If you could design a whole collection of toys, what would it include? Dolls, action figures, puzzles, or something entirely new?

Safety First How would you ensure your toys are safe for children to play with? Think about materials, sizes, and durability.

Skills for Success What skills are important for a successful toy designer—creativity, understanding child development, knowledge of materials, or attention to safety?

Talk to an Expert What would you ask a professional toy designer? "What's the most rewarding part of designing toys?" or "How do you come up with ideas for new toys?" or "What advice would you give to someone wanting to become a toy designer?"

Bonus Activity

Explore the history of popular toys and how they were designed. Ask your teacher or librarian for recommendations on books or documentaries about toy design.

Books:

Movies:

Rate This Profession

On a scale of 1 (not interested) to 10 (dream job), how well does this profession suit your personality and interests?

1   2   3   4   5   6   7   8   9   10

48. CHIROPRACTOR

A chiropractor is a healthcare professional who focuses on diagnosing and treating musculoskeletal issues, particularly those related to the spine. They use hands-on adjustments and manipulations to help relieve pain, improve mobility, and promote overall wellness.

Your Mission – Imagine you're a chiropractor!

Treatment Plan Imagine you're treating a patient with back pain. How would you assess their condition, and what techniques would you use to help them feel better?

Chiropractor's Tools What tools would you use as a chiropractor? Think about tables, adjusters, and other specialized equipment.

A Day in the Life What would your day look like—meeting with patients, performing adjustments, or reviewing x-rays?

Dream Treatment Method If you could create a new treatment method, what would it be? How would it help people improve their health and wellness?

Collaborating with Other Professionals How would you work with doctors, physical therapists, or massage therapists to provide the best care for your patients?

Skills for Success What skills are important for a successful chiropractor—knowledge of anatomy, problem-solving, communication skills, and manual dexterity?

Talk to an Expert What would you ask a professional chiropractor? "What's the most common issue patients come to you for?" or "How do you stay updated on the latest chiropractic techniques?" or "What advice would you give to someone wanting to become a chiropractor?"

Bonus Activity

Learn about the benefits of chiropractic care and how it helps with pain management. Ask for book or video recommendations on chiropractic techniques.

Books:

Movies:

Rate This Profession
On a scale of 1 (not interested) to 10 (dream job), how well does this profession suit your personality and interests?

1   2   3   4   5   6   7   8   9   10

49. DIPLOMAT

A diplomat represents their country in international relations. They work on building peaceful relationships, resolving conflicts, and negotiating treaties or agreements between nations. Diplomats play a crucial role in shaping foreign policies and ensuring their country's interests are protected globally.

Your Mission – Imagine you're a diplomat!

Global Issue Imagine you're negotiating a peace agreement between two countries. What key points would you focus on to ensure both sides feel heard and respected?

Diplomat's Tools What tools would you need as a diplomat—language skills, cultural understanding, negotiation tactics, or international law knowledge?

A Day in the Life What would your day look like—attending meetings, drafting reports, or traveling to different countries to represent your nation?

Dream Diplomatic Mission If you could work on any diplomatic mission, what would it be? Negotiating a world peace agreement or helping solve global environmental issues?

Collaboration How would you work with governments, international organizations, and local communities to foster global cooperation?

Skills for Success What skills are important for a successful diplomat—communication, negotiation, cultural awareness, problem-solving, and adaptability?

Talk to an Expert –What would you ask a professional diplomat? "What's the most challenging part of being a diplomat?" or "How do you handle difficult negotiations?" or "What advice would you give to someone pursuing a career in diplomacy?"

Bonus Activity

Explore global diplomacy and international relations. Ask for book or documentary recommendations about famous diplomats and peace treaties.

Books:

Movies:

Rate This Profession
On a scale of 1 (not interested) to 10 (dream job), how well does this profession suit your personality and interests?

1   2   3   4   5   6   7   8   9   10

50. CRISIS NEGOTIATOR

A crisis negotiator uses communication and psychological tactics to resolve dangerous situations like hostage crises or standoffs peacefully. They work closely with law enforcement to ensure safety and de-escalate high-stress scenarios.

> **Your Mission** – Imagine you're a crisis negotiator!
> **Negotiation Tactics** What strategies would you use to build trust and calm a tense situation?
> **Critical Thinking** How would you assess and respond quickly to ensure safety?
> **Tools for the Job** What tools would you use—communication skills, technology, or teamwork with law enforcement?
> **A Day in the Life** What does your day look like—training, preparing for crises, or handling an active situation?
> **Dream Negotiation** If you could negotiate any crisis, what would it be?
> **Skills for Success** What skills are key for a successful crisis negotiator—emotional control, active listening, and problem-solving?
> **Talk to an Expert** What would you ask a professional crisis negotiator? "What's the most challenging part of the job?" or "How do you manage stress in tense situations?" or "What advice would you give to someone starting in this field?"

Bonus Activity

Learn about real-life crisis negotiators. Ask for recommendations on books or documentaries.

Books:

Movies:

Rate This Profession
On a scale of 1 (not interested) to 10 (dream job), how well does this profession suit your personality and interests?

1 2 3 4 5 6 7 8 9 10

51. DATA ANALYST

A data analyst collects, organizes, and interprets large sets of data to help companies make informed decisions. They use statistical tools and software to find patterns, trends, and insights that guide business strategies.

Your Mission – Imagine you're a data analyst!

Data Collection What kind of data would you analyze—sales data, customer feedback, or maybe social media trends?

Data Tools What software or tools would you use—Excel, SQL, Python, or specialized data analysis programs?

Analyzing Data How would you interpret the data—looking for trends, patterns, or outliers?

A Day in the Life What does your day look like—collecting data, creating reports, or presenting your findings to the team?

Dream Project If you could work on any data project, what would it be—analyzing consumer behavior or predicting market trends?

Skills for Success What skills are important for a data analyst—critical thinking, attention to detail, proficiency in data tools, and problem-solving?

Talk to an Expert – Stay Curious What would you ask a professional data analyst? "What's the most challenging part of analyzing data?" or "How do you ensure the accuracy of your findings?" or "What advice would you give to someone starting in data analysis?"

Bonus Activity
Explore the world of data and learn the basics of analysis. Ask for recommendations on books or tutorials on data analytics.
Books:

Websites:

Rate This Profession
On a scale of 1 (not interested) to 10 (dream job), how well does this profession suit your personality and interests?
1   2   3   4   5   6   7   8   9   10

52. DJ

A DJ (disc jockey) selects and plays music for an audience, typically at events, clubs, or on the radio. DJs mix different songs, create smooth transitions, and set the mood by reading the crowd and adjusting the music accordingly.

Your Mission Imagine you're a DJ!

Create Your Playlist Imagine you're curating a playlist for a big event. What genres or songs would you include? Would you mix old hits with the latest tracks, or keep it all about one style?

DJ Equipment What tools would you need as a DJ? Think about turntables, mixers, headphones, and software. What's essential for creating the perfect mix?

A Day in the Life What would your day look like as a DJ? Would you be preparing your set, rehearsing, or performing at a live event?

Dream Gig If you could DJ any event, what would it be? A music festival, a celebrity party, or a big club night?

Crowd Connection How would you make sure the crowd is enjoying your music? Would you watch their energy, adjust the tempo, or create a specific vibe?

Skills for Success What skills are important for a successful DJ—music knowledge, mixing skills, crowd control, and creativity?

Talk to an Expert What would you ask a professional DJ? "What's your favorite part of performing live?" or "How do you prepare for a big show?" or "What advice would you give to someone starting out as a DJ?"

Bonus Activity
Explore the world of DJing by listening to different mixes and performances. Ask for recommendations on DJ tutorials or music production courses.

Books:

Websites:

Rate This Profession
On a scale of 1 (not interested) to 10 (dream job), how well does this profession suit your personality and interests?

1   2   3   4   5   6   7   8   9   10

53. GEOLOGIST

A geologist studies the Earth's structure, materials, and processes. They examine rocks, minerals, and natural formations to understand how the planet has evolved and how natural events like earthquakes or volcanic eruptions occur. Geologists play a key role in natural resource exploration and environmental protection.

Your Mission Imagine you're a geologist!

Research Project What geological event would you study—earthquakes, volcanoes, or mountain formation?

Fieldwork Tools What tools would you need—rock hammers, maps, GPS, or lab equipment?

A Day in the Life Would you collect rock samples in the field, analyze data in a lab, or write reports?

Dream Discovery Would you want to discover a new mineral, rare fossil, or uncover clues about how continents drifted?

Collaboration How would you work with other experts—environmentalists, engineers, or government officials?

Skills for Success What skills do geologists need—critical thinking, fieldwork skills, research abilities, and Earth science knowledge?

Talk to an Expert – Stay Curious What would you ask a geologist? "What's your most fascinating discovery?" or "How do you prepare for fieldwork in tough environments?" or "What advice would you give to someone pursuing a career in geology?"

Bonus Activity

Learn about famous geological discoveries and Earth's mysteries. Ask for recommendations on documentaries or books on geology.

Books:

Movies:

Rate This Profession
On a scale of 1 (not interested) to 10 (dream job), how well does this profession suit your personality and interests?

1   2   3   4   5   6   7   8   9   10

54. LANDSCAPE ARTIST

A landscape artist creates artwork inspired by nature, capturing scenes like gardens, forests, mountains, or urban spaces using various mediums such as painting, drawing, or digital tools.

Your Mission Imagine you're a landscape artist!

Design Your Landscape Imagine painting a landscape. What would it look like—rolling hills, a beach, or a city park? What colors and textures would you choose?

Inspiration Where do you find inspiration—seasonal changes, specific places, or weather like sunsets or storms?

Artist's Tools What tools would you use—brushes, canvas, pastels, or digital software?

A Day in the Life What's a typical day for you—painting outdoors, sketching in a studio, or editing digital pieces?

Dream Landscape Project If you could create a masterpiece, where would it be displayed—museum, gallery, or public space?

Skills for Success What skills are key for a landscape artist—creativity, attention to detail, love of nature and artistic versatility?

Talk to an Expert – Landscape Artist Q&A

What would you ask a landscape artist? "What's your favorite landscape to create?" or "How do you choose colors and textures?" or "What advice would you give to aspiring landscape artists?"

Bonus Activity

Explore famous landscape artists for inspiration. Ask for book or gallery recommendations.

Books:

Exhibits:

Rate This Profession

On a scale of 1 (not interested) to 10 (dream job), how well does this profession suit your personality and interests?

1 2 3 4 5 6 7 8 9 10

55. CLOWN

A clown entertains with humor, physical comedy, and exaggerated expressions, often performing in circuses, at theaters, or at parties. They wear colorful costumes and face paint, aiming to make people laugh and spread joy.

Your Mission – Imagine you're a clown!

Create Your Character Design your clown persona—what would you look like? Big shoes, a funny nose, or a colorful wig? What's your clown's personality?

Clown Routine What tricks or routines would you perform—juggling, jokes, or slapstick?

Clown Tools What props would you use—balloons, pies, or funny hats?

A Day in the Life What's your day like—preparing costumes, rehearsing, or performing?

Dream Performance Where would you perform—at a circus, theater, or big event?

Skills for Success What skills are key for a clown—creativity, timing, coordination, and humor?

Talk to an Expert What would you ask a professional clown? "What's the funniest thing that happened during a performance?" or "How do you keep your act fresh?" or "What advice would you give to someone who wants to be a clown?"

Bonus Activity

Watch videos of famous clowns for inspiration. Ask for clowning books or documentaries.

Books:

Movies:

Rate This Profession

On a scale of 1 (not interested) to 10 (dream job), how well does this profession suit your personality and interests?

1 2 3 4 5 6 7 8 9 10

56. INSURANCE AGENT

An insurance agent helps people choose insurance plans that protect them from financial loss. They assess clients' needs, explain different types of coverage (like health, life, or car insurance), and help them find the best policies. Insurance agents work for insurance companies or independently.

> **Your Mission** – Imagine you're an insurance agent!
>
> **Choosing Coverage** Imagine you're helping a client select insurance. What kind of coverage would you recommend—life, auto, health, or home?
>
> **Explain Policies** How would you explain a complex policy to a client so they fully understand their coverage?
>
> **A Day in the Life** What would your day look like? Would you meet clients, process claims, or update policies?
>
> **Dream Client** If you could work with any type of client, who would it be? A family, a business, or maybe a celebrity?
>
> **Skills for Success** What skills are important for an insurance agent—communication, problem-solving, attention to detail, and knowledge of insurance policies?
>
> **Talk to an Expert** What would you ask an insurance agent? "What's the most common question clients ask?" or "How do you stay informed about new policies or regulations?" or "What advice would you give to someone interested in becoming an insurance agent?"

Bonus Activity

Explore different types of insurance policies. Ask for recommendations on books or articles about the insurance industry.

Books:

Websites:

Rate This Profession

On a scale of 1 (not interested) to 10 (dream job), how well does this profession suit your personality and interests?

1   2   3   4   5   6   7   8   9   10

57. PODCAST HOST

A podcast host creates and presents audio content on various topics, from entertainment to education. They engage with guests, share stories, and provide insights to entertain or inform their audience.

Your Mission – Imagine you're a podcast host!

Choose Your Topic Imagine you're starting a podcast. What topic would you choose? Would it be interviews, storytelling, news, or perhaps niche hobbies?

Guest Interview Who would your dream guest be, and what questions would you ask them?

Podcast Setup What equipment would you need to create your podcast? Think about microphones, editing software, or maybe even a podcast studio.

A Day in the Life What would your day look like? Would you record episodes, research topics, or interact with your audience on social media?

Skills for Success What skills are important to be a successful podcast host—public speaking, communication, creativity, and editing skills?

Talk to an Expert - What would you ask a professional podcast host? "How do you come up with fresh ideas for episodes?" or "What's the hardest part of hosting a podcast?" or "What advice would you give to someone starting their own podcast?"

Bonus Activity
Listen to different podcasts and analyze their style. What makes them engaging? Ask for recommendations on podcasts you could explore.

Podcasts:

Books:

Rate This Profession
On a scale of 1 (not interested) to 10 (dream job), how well does this profession suit your personality and interests?
1 2 3 4 5 6 7 8 9 10

58. VLOGGER

A vlogger creates and shares video content, typically on platforms like YouTube or social media. Vloggers document daily life, travel, interests, or specific topics, engaging with their audience through storytelling and visuals. They edit their videos, create engaging thumbnails, and build a personal brand to attract viewers.

> **Your Mission** – Imagine you're a vlogger!
>
> **Choose Your Niche** Imagine you're starting a vlog. What would your focus be? Would you share travel adventures, lifestyle tips, gaming, or DIY projects?
>
> **Content Creation** What type of content would you film? Would it be daily vlogs, tutorials, or challenges?
>
> **Filming Setup** What equipment would you need? Think about cameras, lighting, or editing software.
>
> **A Day in the Life** What does a typical day look like for you? Would you be filming, editing, interacting with your followers, or brainstorming new ideas?
>
> **Skills for Success** What skills are important to be a successful vlogger—creativity, editing, storytelling, and audience engagement?
>
> **Talk to an Expert** What would you ask a professional vlogger? "How do you keep your content fresh and exciting?" or "What challenges do you face when creating videos?" or "What advice would you give to someone starting a vlog?"

Bonus Activity
Watch some popular vlogs and analyze what makes them successful. What kind of editing or storytelling do they use?

Vlogs:

Books:

Rate This Profession
On a scale of 1 (not interested) to 10 (dream job), how well does this profession suit your personality and interests?
1 2 3 4 5 6 7 8 9 10

59. BRAND STRATEGIST

A brand strategist helps businesses create and maintain a strong, memorable brand. They develop strategies to promote a company's values, products, and services to connect with their target audience. By researching market trends, analyzing competitors, and building brand identity, they ensure a company stands out and resonates with consumers.

Your Mission – Imagine you're a brand strategist!

Create a Brand Imagine you're designing a new brand. What's its mission, values, and target audience? What makes it unique compared to competitors?

Brand Identity How would you build the brand's visual identity? What colors, logos, and messaging would you use to appeal to your audience?

Market Research What tools would you use to understand customer behavior and market trends—surveys, focus groups, or social media analytics?

A Day in the Life What does your day look like—researching competitors, working with designers, or creating marketing campaigns?

Skills for Success What skills are important to be a successful brand strategist—creativity, market analysis, communication, and the ability to think long-term?

Talk to an Expert – Brand Strategist Q&A What would you ask a professional brand strategist? "How do you develop a brand strategy from scratch?" or "What's the most challenging part of building a brand?" or "What advice would you give to someone starting in brand strategy?"

Bonus Activity
Research successful brands and analyze how they've built their identity.
Books:

Websites:

Rate This Profession
On a scale of 1 (not interested) to 10 (dream job), how well does this profession suit your personality and interests?
1 2 3 4 5 6 7 8 9 10

60. ANTIQUE APPRAISER

An antique appraiser evaluates and estimates the value of antiques and collectibles. They have expertise in various historical items, including furniture, art, jewelry, and rare artifacts. By researching an item's history, condition, and market trends, they provide valuable insights for buying, selling, or insuring items.

Your Mission – Imagine you're an antique appraiser!

Evaluate an Antique Imagine you're appraising an old painting or piece of furniture. What factors would you consider—its age, condition, rarity, or historical significance?

Research Methods What resources would you use to determine the value of an antique—auction records, historical references, or expert consultations?

Tools of the Trade What tools might you need for your job—magnifying glasses, reference books, or digital tools for research?

A Day in the Life What does your day look like—inspecting antiques, meeting with clients, or researching the history of a valuable item?

Skills for Success What skills are important for a successful antique appraiser—attention to detail, knowledge of history, research skills, and a keen eye for value?

Talk to an Expert – Stay Curious What would you ask a professional appraiser? "What's the rarest or most valuable antique you've ever appraised?" or "How do you determine the authenticity of an antique?" or "What advice would you give to someone interested in becoming an appraiser?"

Bonus Activity
Explore antique shops or attend antique auctions to learn more about the appraisal process.
Books:

Websites:

Rate This Profession
On a scale of 1 (not interested) to 10 (dream job),
how well does this profession suit your personality and interests?
1   2   3   4   5   6   7   8   9   10

61. INFLUENCER

An influencer is someone who uses social media to impact opinions, behaviors, or purchasing decisions of their audience. They create content, build personal brands, and collaborate with brands to promote products or causes. Influencers can specialize in fashion, lifestyle, travel, beauty, fitness, and other niches.

Your Mission – Imagine you're an influencer!

Build Your Brand Imagine you're creating your own personal brand. What kind of content would you focus on—lifestyle, fashion, tech, or fitness? What platform would you use—Instagram, YouTube, or TikTok?

Engage Your Audience How would you keep your followers engaged? Would you share behind-the-scenes content, tutorials, or personal stories?

Collaboration With Brands If a brand approached you for a partnership, how would you decide if it fits with your values and brand?

A Day in the Life What does your day look like as an influencer—shooting content, responding to followers, or attending events?

Skills for Success What skills are important for a successful influencer—creativity, authenticity, social media savvy, or the ability to connect with others?

Talk to an Expert – What would you ask a professional influencer? "How do you stay authentic while promoting brands?" or "What advice would you give to someone starting their influencer career?" or "How do you manage the pressures of social media?"

Bonus Activity
Research some top influencers and their rise to fame. Ask for recommendations on books, documentaries, or interviews to learn more.
Books:

Websites:

Rate This Profession
On a scale of 1 (not interested) to 10 (dream job), how well does this profession suit your personality and interests?
1 2 3 4 5 6 7 8 9 10

62. FARMER

A farmer is someone who cultivates land, raises animals, and produces food, fiber, or other agricultural products. They work with crops like vegetables, grains, or fruits, and may also manage livestock. Farmers use knowledge of the land, weather, and technology to grow and harvest products that feed communities.

> **Your Mission** – Imagine you're a farmer!
>
> **Plan Your Farm** Imagine you're planning your farm. What would you grow—corn, wheat, vegetables, or fruits? Would you raise animals too?
>
> **Farm Tools** What tools would you need—tractors, plows, irrigation systems, or maybe greenhouses?
>
> **A Day in the Life** What would your day look like—planting seeds, tending to animals, or harvesting crops?
>
> **Sustainable Farming** If you could implement any sustainable farming practice, what would it be—using renewable energy, rotating crops, or reducing pesticide use?
>
> **Skills for Success** What skills are important for a successful farmer—problem-solving, knowledge of agriculture, physical strength, or the ability to adapt to changing conditions?
>
> **Talk to an Expert** What would you ask a professional farmer? "What's the biggest challenge you face in farming?" or "How do you adapt to changes in weather or market demand?" or "What advice would you give to someone interested in farming?"

Bonus Activity
Learn more about farming and agricultural practices. Ask for recommendations on books or documentaries about the industry.
Books:

Movies:

Rate This Profession
On a scale of 1 (not interested) to 10 (dream job), how well does this profession suit your personality and interests?
1   2   3   4   5   6   7   8   9   10

63. INTERPLANETARY LAWYER

An interplanetary lawyer is a legal professional who works with laws and regulations related to space exploration, interplanetary travel, and the colonization of other planets. They may handle cases involving space treaties, planetary rights, extraterrestrial resources, or the legal aspects of intergalactic businesses.

Your Mission – Imagine you're an interplanetary lawyer!

Create a Space Treaty Imagine you're drafting a treaty between Earth and a colony on Mars. What would the treaty include—resource sharing, space traffic regulations, or environmental protection?

Space Law Case You're defending a company accused of illegal mining on an asteroid. What evidence would you use, and how would you argue the case?

A Day in the Life What would your day look like—reviewing interplanetary treaties, advising space agencies, or negotiating contracts for space missions?

Future of Space Law If you could shape the future of space law, what changes would you make—improving space governance, human rights for astronauts, or protecting extraterrestrial life?

Skills for Success What skills are essential for a successful interplanetary lawyer—strong legal knowledge, problem-solving, negotiation or understanding space science and technology?

Talk to an Expert (It will not be easy to find one.) "What's the most complex issue you face in space law?" or "How do you stay informed about space-related developments?" or "What advice would you give someone interested in space law?"

Bonus Activity

Explore the growing field of space law and its challenges. Ask for recommendations on books, movies, or articles related to the topic.

Books:

Movies:

Rate This Profession

On a scale of 1 (not interested) to 10 (dream job), how well does this profession suit your personality and interests?

1 2 3 4 5 6 7 8 9 10

64. SOCIAL MEDIA MANAGER

A social media manager creates, curates, and manages content across various social media platforms. They help brands build an online presence, engage with audiences, and drive traffic or sales. They also analyze data to optimize strategies and improve engagement.

Your Mission – Imagine you're a social media manager!

Create a Content Calendar Imagine you're planning content for the month. What type of posts would you create—educational, promotional, or interactive? How often would you post?

Engagement Strategy You're working on a strategy to grow your brand following. Would you focus on influencer partnerships, contests, or live events?

Analyzing Metrics What tools would you use to measure the success of your posts—likes, shares, comments, or website traffic?

Crisis Management What would you do if there was negative feedback on a post? How would you handle it, and how would you protect brand reputation?

Skills for Success What skills are important for a successful social media manager—creativity, communication, time management, and knowledge of analytics?

Talk to an Expert – What would you ask a social media manager? "How do you stay updated on social media trends?" or "What's the most challenging part of managing brand social presence?" or "What advice would you give to someone starting out in social media management?"

Bonus Activity

Explore social media marketing strategies and trends. Ask for recommendations on books, blogs, or online courses.

Books:

Websites:

Rate This Profession
On a scale of 1 (not interested) to 10 (dream job), how well does this profession suit your personality and interests?
1 2 3 4 5 6 7 8 9 10

65. RENEWABLE ENERGY EXPERT

A renewable energy expert specializes in developing and implementing sustainable energy solutions. They work with technologies like solar, wind, hydro, and geothermal to reduce dependence on fossil fuels and help protect the environment.

Your Mission – Imagine you're a renewable energy expert!

Design Your Green Energy Plan Imagine you're tasked with creating a renewable energy plan for a city. What types of renewable energy would you use—solar panels, wind turbines, or hydroelectric power?

Energy Efficiency Challenge How would you improve the energy efficiency of a building? Would you suggest better insulation, smart thermostats, or installing solar panels?

Research Project What environmental issues would you focus on solving—reducing carbon emissions, increasing renewable energy adoption, or advancing energy storage technology?

A Day in the Life What would your day look like? Would you be analyzing data, designing energy systems, or meeting with companies about new energy solutions?

Skills for Success What skills are crucial for success in renewable energy—technical knowledge, problem-solving, innovation, and an understanding of environmental impact?

Talk to an Expert – What would you ask a renewable energy expert? Maybe, "What's the biggest challenge in developing renewable energy technologies?" or "How do you stay updated on new advancements in the industry?" or "What advice would you give to someone interested in renewable energy?"

Bonus Activity

Explore sustainable energy solutions and technologies. Ask for recommendations on books or documentaries about renewable energy.
Books:

Movies:

Rate This Profession
On a scale of 1 (not interested) to 10 (dream job), how well does this profession suit your personality and interests?
1   2   3   4   5   6   7   8   9   10

66. WASTE MANAGEMENT ENGINEER

A waste management engineer focuses on developing systems and technologies to manage waste efficiently and sustainably. They work to reduce, recycle, and safely dispose of waste materials, ensuring environmental protection and compliance with regulations.

>**Your Mission** – Imagine you're a waste management engineer!
>
>**Waste Reduction Plan** Imagine you're tasked with reducing waste in a city. What strategies would you implement—more recycling, composting, or waste-to-energy plants?
>
>**Innovative Solutions** What new technologies would you use to improve waste management—robotic sorting, advanced recycling methods, or sustainable landfill designs?
>
>**A Day in the Life** - What would your day look like? Would you be designing waste management systems, analyzing environmental impacts, or collaborating with local governments to improve waste practices?
>
>**Environmental Impact** - How would you measure the environmental impact of your waste management solutions—by tracking carbon emissions, waste diversion rates, or water contamination?
>
>**Skills for Success** What skills are key for success in waste management engineering—technical knowledge, problem-solving, environmental awareness, and project management?
>
>**Talk to an Expert – What would you ask a waste management engineer?** "What are the most effective strategies for reducing landfill waste?" or "What innovations do you think will shape the future of waste management?" or "What advice would you give to someone interested in this field?"

Bonus Activity

Explore current waste management practices and innovations. Ask for recommendations on books or documentaries about recycling.

Books:

Other resources:

Rate This Profession

On a scale from 1 (not interested) to 10 (dream job), how well does this profession suit your personality?

1 2 3 4 5 6 7 8 9 10

67. DRONE OPERATOR

A drone operator uses unmanned aerial vehicles (UAVs) to capture images, videos, and data from the sky. They work in various fields such as photography, surveying, agriculture, or search and rescue, ensuring the drone operates safely and efficiently.

Your Mission – Imagine you're a drone operator!

Drone Flight Plan Imagine you're planning a drone flight. What's the purpose—capturing a video, surveying land, or inspecting infrastructure? What route and altitude would you choose?

Drone Features What type of drone would you use? Think about camera quality, battery life, and stability. How would those features impact your work?

A Day in the Life What would your day look like? Would you fly drones for aerial photography, mapping, or delivering supplies? What tasks would you handle on-site?

Drone Safety What safety protocols would you follow while operating a drone—pre-flight checks, avoiding restricted areas, or managing battery power?

Skills for Success What skills are key for a drone operator—technical knowledge, attention to detail, problem-solving, or the ability to operate drones under various conditions?

Talk to an Expert – What would you ask a drone operator? "What's the most exciting project you've worked on?" or "What challenges do you face when flying drones?" or "What advice would you give someone interested in becoming a drone operator?"

Bonus Activity

Explore the world of drone technology and its applications. Ask for recommendations for books or documentaries about drones and their uses.

Books:

Movies:

Rate This Profession

On a scale of 1 (not interested) to 10 (dream job), how well does this profession suit your personality and interests?

1   2   3   4   5   6   7   8   9   10

68. CRYPTOCURRENCY TRADER

A cryptocurrency trader buys and sells digital currencies like Bitcoin, Ethereum, or others to make a profit. They analyze market trends, track prices and make quick decisions based on market conditions to maximize returns.

Your Mission – Imagine You're a Cryptocurrency Trader!

Trading Strategy
Imagine you're making your next trade. What strategy would you use—short-term trading, long-term investing, or day trading? How would you choose the right cryptocurrency to invest in?

Market Analysis What tools or methods would you use to analyze the market—charts, news, or technical indicators? How would you predict price movements?

A Day in the Life What does your day look like? Would you be monitoring market changes, placing trades, or analyzing trends? How do you stay updated on the latest news?

Risk Management How would you manage risk in your trades? Would you use stop-loss orders, diversify investments, or limit your exposure to certain coins?

Skills for Success What skills are important for a successful cryptocurrency trader—market analysis, quick decision-making, financial knowledge, and emotional discipline?

Talk to an Expert – What would you ask a professional trader? "What's the most important thing to focus on when trading cryptocurrencies?" or "How do you stay calm during volatile market changes?" or "What advice would you give someone starting to trade cryptocurrencies?"

Bonus Activity
Explore the world of cryptocurrency and blockchain technology. Ask for recommendations on books or websites to understand how it works.
Books:

Websites:

Rate This Profession
On a scale of 1 (not interested) to 10 (dream job), how well does this profession suit your personality and interests?
1 2 3 4 5 6 7 8 9 10

69. ARTIFICIAL INTELLIGENCE TRAINER

An AI trainer teaches machines how to recognize patterns, understand data, and make decisions by feeding it vast amounts of data to improve learning algorithms. It ensures AI systems to become smarter and more efficient, often working with data scientists and engineers.

Your Mission – Imagine you're an AI trainer!

Training Data Imagine you're training a new AI model. What kind of data would you feed it—text, images, or audio? How would you ensure the data is accurate and diverse?

Algorithm Selection What algorithms would you use to train your AI—neural networks, decision trees, or reinforcement learning? How do you decide which is best?

A Day on the Job What does your day look like? Would you be cleaning data, adjusting algorithms, or testing models to see how well they perform?

Improving AI How would you evaluate an AI system's performance? What metrics would you use, and how would you improve it if it underperforms?

Skills for Success What skills are important for an AI trainer—data analysis, understanding machine learning algorithms, coding skills, and problem-solving?

Talk to an Expert – What would you ask a professional AI trainer? "What's the biggest challenge you face when training an AI?" or "How do you ensure your AI is learning in a fair and unbiased way?" or "What advice would you give to someone looking to become an AI trainer?"

Bonus Activity

Explore the world of artificial intelligence and machine learning. Ask for recommendations on books or websites to learn more about AI.
Books:

Websites:

Rate This Profession

On a scale of 1 (not interested) to 10 (dream job), how well does this profession suit your personality and interests?

1 2 3 4 5 6 7 8 9 10

70. MARTIAL ARTS TEACHER

A martial arts teacher trains students in various disciplines of martial arts, teaching techniques for self-defense, discipline, fitness, and mental focus. They may specialize in styles like karate, kung fu, taekwondo, judo, or Brazilian jiu-jitsu, to help students grow physically and mentally.

Your Mission – Imagine you're a martial arts teacher!

Training Session Imagine you're leading a class. What techniques would you teach—basic stances, self-defense moves, or advanced forms? How would you explain them clearly?

Student Progress How would you assess your students' progress? Would you use sparring, belt testing, or other techniques to track their development?

A Day in the Life What does your day look like? Would you be preparing lesson plans, demonstrating techniques, or mentoring students in and out of class?

Class Environment How would you create a safe encouraging environment for your students to learn and improve?

Skills for Success What skills are important for a martial arts teacher—patience, leadership, strong knowledge of techniques, or the ability to motivate others?

Talk to an Expert – What would you ask a professional martial arts teacher? Maybe, "What's the most rewarding part of teaching martial arts?" or "How do you motivate students who are struggling with techniques?" or "What advice would you give to someone who wants to teach martial arts?"

Bonus Activity
Explore different martial arts styles and their histories. Ask for recommendations on books or documentaries about martial arts.
Books:

Movies:

Rate This Profession
On a scale of 1 (not interested) to 10 (dream job), how well does this profession suit your personality and interests?

1 2 3 4 5 6 7 8 9 10

71. SPIRITUAL LEADER

A spiritual leader offers guidance and support to individuals or communities seeking growth, inner peace, and connection with the divine. They may come from various traditions—Christianity, Buddhism, Hinduism, or New Age practices and provide teachings, meditation, and personal mentorship.

Your Mission – Imagine you're a spiritual leader!

Guiding Principles You're leading a spiritual retreat—what core teachings would you focus on? Mindfulness, compassion, or self-discovery? How would you help others connect with their higher selves?

Spiritual Practice Would you lead meditation, prayer, or rituals? How would you support people on their personal spiritual journeys?

A Day in the Life What does your day look like? Are you meditating, offering counseling, or leading group sessions?

Building Inner Peace How would you help people find balance and peace, especially during challenging times?

Skills for Success What skills matter most—empathy, spiritual knowledge, communication, or the ability to inspire others?

Talk to an Expert If you could ask a spiritual leader anything, what would it be? "How do you maintain your own spiritual practice while helping others?" or "What's the most rewarding part of guiding others?" or "What advice would you give to someone interested in becoming a spiritual leader?"

Bonus Activity
Explore different spiritual paths. Ask for book or documentary recommendations to learn more.
Books:

Movies:

Rate This Profession
On a scale of 1 (not interested) to 10 (dream job), how well does this profession suit your personality and interests?
1 2 3 4 5 6 7 8 9 10

72. ROBOTICS ENGINEER

A robotics engineer designs, builds, and tests robots and automated systems. They combine engineering, computer science, and technology to create robots that can perform tasks, from manufacturing to surgery.

Your Mission – Imagine You're a Robotics Engineer!

Design Your Robot Imagine designing a robot. What would it do—assist with household chores, explore space, or help in healthcare? What features would it have?

Engineering Challenge What materials and technology would you use to build your robot? Think about sensors, motors, and artificial intelligence.

Robot's Tools What tools or equipment would you use—CAD software, 3D printers, or assembly tools?

A Day in the Life What would your day look like—designing parts, testing prototypes, or troubleshooting issues?

Dream Robotics Project If you could work on any robot project, what would it be—creating a robot for space exploration, developing a robot assistant, or building a humanoid robot?

Skills for Success What skills are important—problem-solving, coding, engineering knowledge, and creativity?

Talk to an xpert - What would you ask a robotics engineer? "What's the most exciting project you've worked on?" "How do you overcome challenges in robot design?" "What advice would you give to someone wanting to become a robotics engineer?"

Bonus Activity

Learn more about groundbreaking robots and technologies. Ask for books or documentaries about robotics.

Books:

Movies:

Rate This Profession

On a scale of 1 (not interested) to 10 (dream job), how well does this profession suit your personality and interests?

1 2 3 4 5 6 7 8 9 10

73. AUGMENTED REALITY DESIGNER

An augmented reality (AR) designer creates digital experiences that blend real and virtual worlds. From games and educational tools to interactive shopping and marketing, AR designers use technology to make digital content part of our everyday surroundings. Their work combines creativity with technical skills to design fun, useful, engaging experiences.

Your Mission – Imagine you're an AR designer!

Design Your AR Experience What kind of AR experience would you create? A learning tool, a virtual home decorator, or an outdoor adventure game?

Design Challenge What tools and technologies would you use—Unity, ARKit, or ARCore? Would your project run on smartphones, tablets, or AR glasses?

AR Design Tools What creative software would you need—3D modeling programs, design platforms, or coding tools?

A Day in the Life What would a typical day look like? Would you brainstorm ideas, design 3D objects, test interactions, or work with developers and artists?

Dream AR Project If you could create any AR project, what would it be—a historical time travel app, a virtual playground, or a futuristic classroom?

Skills for Success What skills do you think are important—creativity, coding, 3D design, and spatial thinking?

Talk to an Expert – What would you ask AR Designer? "What's the most exciting project you've worked on?" or "What's the hardest part of designing for both digital and physical worlds?" or "What advice would you give to someone interested in AR design?"

Bonus Activity
Check out videos or articles about how AR is used in fields like healthcare, fashion, or sports. See how technology and creativity come together!
Websites:

Other resources:

Rate This Profession
On a scale of 1 (not interested) to 10 (dream job), how well does this profession suit your personality and interests?
1 2 3 4 5 6 7 8 9 10

74. ELECTRIC VEHICLE DESIGNER

An electric vehicle (EV) designer focuses on creating sustainable, efficient, innovative electric vehicles. They work on designing vehicle systems, structures, and components like battery packs, motors, and charging systems to optimize performance, range, and user experience.

Your Mission Imagine you're an EV designer!

Design Your EV What kind of electric vehicle would you create? A high-performance sports car, an eco-friendly city car, or an SUV?

Design Challenge What materials and technologies would you use? Think about lightweight materials, energy-efficient motors, and long-lasting battery technologies.

EV Design Tools What tools would you use—CAD software for vehicle design, simulation software for battery performance, or 3D printing for prototyping?

A Day in the Life What would your day look like—designing vehicle components, testing prototypes, or troubleshooting issues with performance?

Dream EV Project If you could work on any EV project, what would it be—a groundbreaking new electric car model, an autonomous EV system, or a sustainable vehicle for mass transportation?

Skills for Success What skills are important? Engineering knowledge, problem-solving, proficiency in CAD software, understanding of electric drivetrains, and a passion for sustainability are key.

Talk to an Expert – Stay Curious What would you ask an EV designer? "What's the most exciting EV technology you've worked on?" or "How do you ensure the balance between performance and energy efficiency in electric vehicles?" or "What advice would you give to someone wanting to become an EV designer?"

Bonus Activity

Ask your teacher or librarian for books or documentaries about innovative electric vehicles, renewable energy, and future transportation.

Books:

Movie:

Rate This Profession

On a scale of 1 (not interested) to 10 (dream job), how well does this profession suit your personality and interests?

1 2 3 4 5 6 7 8 9 10

75. MEMORY IMPLANT SPECIALIST (NEUROTECHNOLOGIST)

A memory implant specialist designs neural technologies to enhance, restore, or modify memory, merging neuroscience, biotech, and engineering.

Your Mission – Imagine you're a memory implant specialist!
Design Your Memory Implant What would your implant do—help restore lost memories, enhance memory retention, or provide memory augmentation for learning and productivity?
Design Challenge What technologies and materials would you use? Think about neurostimulation, biocompatible materials, brain-computer interfaces (BCIs), and data storage systems.
Implant Tools What tools would you use—neuroscience labs for brain mapping, 3D printers for implant prototypes, or AI software to simulate neural interactions?
A Day in the Life What would your day look like—researching new memory technologies, testing neural interfaces, or working with patients to monitor the implant's effects?
Dream Memory Project If you could work on any project, what would it be— would you develop memory enhancers, aid Alzheimer's patients, or advance BCIs for cognition?
Skills for Success Neuroscience knowledge, biomedical engineering, coding for neuroprosthetics, data analysis, and problem-solving in complex biological systems are essential.
Talk to an Expert – Memory Implant Specialist
"What's the most advanced memory tech you've worked on?" or "How do you ensure brain safety?" or "Any advice for future memory implant specialists?"

Bonus Activity
Search for books or documentaries about how the brain works, memory research, and futuristic brain implants.
Books:

Movie:

Rate This Profession
On a scale of 1 (not interested) to 10 (dream job), how well does this profession suit your personality and interests?
1 2 3 4 5 6 7 8 9 10

76. DREAM AUGMENTATION SPECIALIST

A dream augmentation specialist creates technologies to enhance, influence, or guide dreams. This field blends neuroscience, psychology, and technology to improve sleep, treat disorders, and boost creativity through dream manipulation.

> **Your Mission** – Imagine you're a dream augmentation specialist!
> **Design Your Technology** Would your technology enhance lucid dreams, stop nightmares, or spark creative problem-solving dreams?
> **Design Challenge** What tools would you use—brainwave monitors, neural stimulators, or sleep trackers?
> **Augmentation Tools** Would you rely on EEG devices, dream analysis software, or neurostimulation tech?
> **A Day in the Life** Would you study brain activity, design new devices, or test dream interventions?
> **Dream Project** Would you create dream-controlling devices, PTSD therapies, or tools to boost creativity?
> **Skills for Success** Key skills: neuroscience, sleep science, neurotechnology and creative problem-solving.
> **Talk to an Expert – Dream Augmentation Specialist** "What's the coolest dream tech you've worked on?" or "How do you safely influence brain activity?" or "What advice would you give future dream specialists?"

Bonus Activity
Explore dream science! Ask your teacher or librarian for books or documentaries on sleep science, lucid dreaming, and future dream technology.
Books:

Other Resources:

Rate This Profession
On a scale of 1 (not interested) to 10 (dream job), how well does this profession suit your personality and interests?
1   2   3   4   5   6   7   8   9   10

77. REAL ESTATE AGENT

A real estate agent helps people buy, sell, or rent properties. They provide expertise on the housing market, guide clients through the transaction process, and negotiate deals. They may specialize in residential, commercial, or industrial real estate.

Your Mission – Imagine you're a real estate agent!

Design Your Real Estate Service What kind of real estate service would you offer—luxury homes, first-time buyer assistance, or commercial property leasing?

Design Challenge What tools and technologies would you use? Think about property listing platforms, virtual tours, market analysis tools, and CRM systems for client management.

Agent Tools What tools would you use—real estate apps for listings, contract management software, or digital marketing strategies?

A Day in the Life What would your day look like—showing properties, negotiating deals, or managing paperwork?

Dream Project If you could work on any real estate project, what would it be—finding properties for a high-profile client, building a real estate portfolio, or developing a new housing community?

Skills for Success What skills are important? Strong communication, negotiation skills, market knowledge, time management, and understanding of real estate laws and contracts are essential.

Talk to an Expert – Real Estate Agent "What's the most rewarding part of being a real estate agent?" or "How do you handle challenges like market fluctuations or difficult negotiations?" or "What advice would you give to someone wanting to become a real estate agent?"

Bonus Activity

Explore the world of real estate! Ask for books or documentaries about buying and selling homes, famous properties, or how cities are planned and built.

Books:

Other Resources:

Rate This Profession

On a scale of 1 (not interested) to 10 (dream job), how well does this profession suit your personality and interests?

1 2 3 4 5 6 7 8 9 10

78. FINANCIAL ADVISOR

A financial advisor helps individuals and businesses make informed decisions about their finances. They offer advice on investments, savings, retirement planning, insurance, taxes, and overall financial management to help clients achieve their financial goals.

Your Mission – Imagine you're a financial advisor!

Design Your Financial Services What kind of financial services would you offer—retirement planning, investment strategies, tax planning, or wealth management?

Design Challenge What tools and technologies would you use? Think about financial planning software, investment analysis tools, or budgeting apps.

Advisor Tools What tools would you use—financial calculators, portfolio management software, or CRM systems for client tracking?

A Day in the Life What would your day look like—meeting clients, creating financial plans, researching investment opportunities, or reviewing market trends?

Dream Project If you could work on any financial project, what would it be—helping a client achieve financial independence, managing a major investment fund, or advising a startup on its financial strategy?

Skills for Success What skills are important? Analytical skills, understanding financial markets, knowledge of investment strategies, communication skills, and the ability to build trust with clients are key.

Talk to an Expert – Financial Advisor "What's the most rewarding part of being a financial advisor?" or "How do you handle market volatility or financial uncertainties with clients?" or "What advice would you give to someone wanting to become a financial advisor?"

Bonus Activity

Learn more how money works! Ask your teacher or librarian for books or documentaries about saving, investing, and building smart money habits.
Books:

Other Resources:

Rate This Profession
On a scale of 1 (not interested) to 10 (dream job), how well does this profession suit your personality and interests?

1 2 3 4 5 6 7 8 9 10

79. LABORATORY RESEARCH SPECIALIST

A laboratory research specialist designs, conducts, and analyzes experiments to advance scientific knowledge. They work in various fields such as chemistry, biology, physics, and engineering, using controlled environments to validate theories, test hypotheses, and discover new insights.

Your Mission – Imagine you're a laboratory research specialist!

Design Your Experiment What kind of experiments would you design—studying chemical reactions, exploring biological processes, or testing new materials?

Design Challenge What tools and technologies would you use? Think about lab equipment (microscopes, centrifuges, spectrometers) or software for data analysis and simulation.

Research Tools What tools would you use—precision measuring instruments, data analysis software, or safety equipment for hazardous materials?

A Day in the Life What would your day look like—setting up experiments, analyzing data, documenting findings, or troubleshooting challenges in ongoing research?

Dream Experiment If you could work on any research project, what would it be—creating a new medical treatment, discovering a new element, or advancing sustainable energy technologies?

Skills for Success What skills are important? Analytical thinking, attention to detail, problem-solving, and data analysis are key.

Questions for a Laboratory Research Specialist

"What's the most exciting experiment you've ever worked on?" or "How do you ensure the accuracy and reliability of your experimental results?" or "What advice would you give to someone wanting to become a laboratory research specialist?"

Bonus Activity

Explore the exciting world of scientific research! Ask your teacher or librarian for books about lab discoveries, famous experiments, and how research helps solve real-world problems.

Books:

Other Resources:

Rate This Profession

On a scale from 1 (not interested) to 10 (dream job), how well does this profession suit your personality?

1 2 3 4 5 6 7 8 9 10

80. DRIVER

A driver operates various types of vehicles, transporting people, goods, or materials from one location to another. Drivers work in many sectors, including transportation, logistics, delivery services, and public transit, ensuring safety and efficiency on the road.

Your Mission – Imagine you're a driver!

Design Your Driving Service What type of driving service would you offer—long-distance transportation, delivery services, or public transit?

Design Challenge What tools and technologies would you use? Think about GPS systems, route planning software, or electric vehicles for eco-friendly driving.

Driving Tools What tools would you use—vehicle maintenance tools, traffic monitoring apps, or driver safety technology like dash cams?

A Day in the Life What would your day look like—driving routes, handling traffic, delivering goods, or assisting passengers?

Dream Driving Job If you could work in any driving role, what would it be—driving a luxury car, managing a fleet of electric vehicles, or working in autonomous vehicle testing?

Skills for Success What skills are important? Safe driving skills, knowledge of road laws, good time management, navigation skills, and the ability to handle unexpected situations are essential.

Talk to an Expert "What's the most rewarding part of being a driver?" or "How do you stay focused and safe during long driving hours?" or "What advice would you give to someone wanting to become a driver?"

Bonus Activity
Learn more about transportation and the skills drivers need! Ask your teacher or librarian for books or documentaries about vehicles, road safety, and how transportation shapes our world.
Books:

Other Resources:

Rate This Profession
On a scale of 1 (not interested) to 10 (dream job), how well does this profession suit your personality and interests?
1   2   3   4   5   6   7   8   9   10

81. FLORIST

A florist is a professional who designs, arranges, and sells flowers for various occasions like weddings, funerals, holidays, and special events. They use their creativity to create beautiful, personalized floral arrangements.

Your Mission – Imagine you're a florist!

Design Your Floral Service What type of floral arrangements would you create—wedding bouquets, holiday centerpieces, or unique arrangements for special occasions?

Design Challenge What tools and materials would you use? Think about flower varieties, floral foam, vases, and ribbon, or specialized tools for cutting and arranging flowers.

Floral Tools What tools would you use—scissors, floral tape, floral wire, or refrigeration systems to keep flowers fresh?

A Day in the Life What would your day look like—designing new arrangements, interacting with customers, maintaining flower stock, or setting up events?

Dream Floral Project If you could work on any floral project, what would it be—designing a grand floral display for a major event, creating custom floral designs for a famous brand, or growing your own flower farm?

Skills for Success What skills are important? Creativity, attention to detail, knowledge of different flower types, design skills, customer service, and an understanding of flower care are key.

Talk to an Expert – Florist "What's the most memorable floral arrangement you've ever made?" or "How do you deal with seasonal changes in flower availability?" or "What advice would you give to someone wanting to become a florist?"

Bonus Activity

Dive into the beauty of flowers and floral design! Ask your teacher or librarian for books or documentaries about flower arrangements, plant care, and the art of floristry.

Books:

Other Resources:

Rate This Profession

On a scale of 1 (not interested) to 10 (dream job), how well does this profession suit your personality and interests?

1   2   3   4   5   6   7   8   9   10

82. SECURITY GUARD

A security guard protects property, people, and assets by monitoring and responding to security threats in places like offices, malls, and events.

Your Mission – Imagine you're a security guard!

Design Your Role What kind of security services would you offer—monitoring high-security buildings, events, or patrolling retail stores?

Design Challenge What tools would you use—surveillance cameras, alarm systems, or access control software?

Security Tools Would you use radios, body cameras, or security systems for monitoring?

A Day in the Life Would you patrol areas, respond to incidents, keep records, or interact with the public to ensure safety?

Dream Project What security project would you choose—designing a system for high-profile locations, managing security at events, or creating new tech to prevent breaches?

Skills for Success Key skills: attention to detail, communication, vigilance, problem-solving, fitness, and knowledge of security protocols.

Talk to an Expert – Questions for a Security Guard "What's the toughest situation you've faced?" or "How do you handle emergencies?" or "Any advice for aspiring security guards?"

Bonus Activity

Explore the world of security and safety! Ask your teacher or librarian for books or documentaries about protecting people, security systems, and the importance of safety in various environments.

Books:

Other Resources:

Rate This Profession
On a scale of 1 (not interested) to 10 (dream job), how well does this profession suit your personality and interests?
1 2 3 4 5 6 7 8 9 10

83. CHILDREN'S RECREATION SPECIALIST

A recreation specialist designs, organizes, and oversees recreational activities and programs for children. They work in schools, community centers, and camps, creating fun, educational, and safe experiences that promote physical activity, creativity, and social development.

Your Mission – Imagine you're a recreation specialist for children!

Design Your Program What kind of recreational programs would you offer—sports leagues, art workshops, after-school activities, or outdoor adventures?

Design Challenge Think about sports equipment, art supplies, or safety protocols for group activities, what resources would you use?

Program Tools What tools would you use—event planning software, activity guides, or child safety gear?

A Day in the Life What would your day look like—planning events, leading activities, ensuring child safety, or working with parents and staff to organize programs?

Dream Project If you could create any recreational program, what would it be—a summer camp focused on nature, an inclusive sports league, or an educational play program for early childhood?

Skills for Success What skills are important? Creativity, leadership, communication, organization, child development knowledge, and the ability to manage groups are key.

Talk to an Expert – Recreation Specialist for Children's Programs "What's the most rewarding part of working with children in recreational programs?" or "How do you ensure safety and inclusivity in your programs?" or "What advice would you give to someone wanting to become a recreation specialist for children?"

Bonus Activity

Learn about fun activities for kids and how recreation helps them grow! Ask your teacher or librarian for books or documentaries about child development, outdoor activities, and creating engaging programs for kids.
Books:

Other Resources:

Rate This Profession
On a scale of 1 (not interested) to 10 (dream job), how well does this profession suit your personality and interests?
1   2   3   4   5   6   7   8   9   10

84. SENIOR CITIZEN RESOURCE CONSULTANT

A senior citizen resource consultant specializes in assisting older adults with various needs, including healthcare, housing, financial planning, and social services. They work with seniors to help them navigate resources and improve their quality of life as they age.

> **Your Mission** – Imagine you're a senior citizen resource consultant!
> **Design Your Services** What services would you offer—retirement planning, assisted living options, or connecting seniors to healthcare?
> **Design Challenge** What tools would you use—databases, communication tools, or healthcare networks?
> **Consulting Tools** Would you use online directories, financial planning software, or community outreach programs?
> **A Day in the Life** Would your day involve consulting seniors, researching resources, or organizing community events?
> **Dream Project** What project would you choose—creating a senior resource guide, developing a wellness program, or improving eldercare services?
> **Skills for Success** Necessary skills: empathy, communication, knowledge of senior services, problem-solving, and project management.
> **Talk to an Expert – Senior People's Resource Consultant Q&A**
> "What's the most rewarding part of helping seniors?" or "How do you stay updated on resources and programs?" or "Any advice for aspiring consultants?"

Bonus Activity
Explore the world of senior care and resources! Ask your teacher or librarian for books or documentaries about aging, senior care, and programs that support older adults.
Books:

Other Resources:

Rate This Profession
On a scale of 1 (not interested) to 10 (dream job), how well does this profession suit your personality and interests?
1 2 3 4 5 6 7 8 9 10

85. EPIDEMIOLOGIST

An epidemiologist studies the distribution, patterns, and causes of diseases and health conditions in populations. They investigate outbreaks, analyze health trends, and use data to recommend public health strategies and interventions to improve community health.

> **Your Mission** – Imagine you're an epidemiologist!
>
> **Design Your Research Focus** What would you study—infectious diseases, environmental health, or chronic diseases?
>
> **Design Challenge** What tools would you use—statistical software, data collection tools, or lab equipment?
>
> **Epidemiology Tools** Would you use surveillance systems, health databases, or GIS for mapping disease?
>
> **A Day in the Life** Would your day involve data collection, trend analysis, fieldwork, or reporting findings?
>
> **Dream Project** What public health initiative would you lead—investigating an outbreak, developing prevention strategies, or conducting a global survey?
>
> **Skills for Success** Key skills: analytical thinking, biostatistics, research abilities, attention to detail, and public health understanding.
>
> **Talk to an Expert – Explore further, ask questions**
> "What's the most impactful research you've done?" or "How do you handle emerging health crises?" or "Any advice for aspiring epidemiologists?"

Bonus Activity

Learn about diseases and public health! Ask your teacher or librarian for books or documentaries on how diseases spread, public health efforts, and the role of epidemiologists.

Books:

Other Resources:

Rate This Profession

On a scale of 1 (not interested) to 10 (dream job), how well does this profession suit your personality and interests?

1   2   3   4   5   6   7   8   9   10

86. SOUND DESIGNER

A sound designer creates, manipulates, and arranges audio elements for various media, such as films, video games, theater, and music. They work to create the perfect auditory experience by designing sound effects, ambiance, and sometimes music to enhance storytelling and user experience.

> **Your Mission** – Imagine you're a sound designer!
>
> **Design Your Soundscape** What projects would you work on—sound effects for games, film audio design, or commercials?
>
> **Design Challenge** What tools would you use—audio editing software, microphones, or field recording equipment?
>
> **Sound Design Tools** Would you use a DAW (digital audio workstation), synthesizers, or sound libraries to create effects and music?
>
> **A Day in the Life** Would you spend your day recording sound, editing audio, mixing soundtracks, or collaborating with directors?
>
> **Dream Project** What would your dream project be—designing audio for a blockbuster, creating VR game sound, or scoring a play?
>
> **Skills for Success** Key skills: creativity, technical sound editing, attention to detail, familiarity with software, and understanding sound's emotional impact.
>
> **Talk to an Expert – Sound Designer Q&A** "What's the most memorable project you've worked on?" or "How do you match sounds to emotional tones?" or "Any advice for aspiring sound designers?"

Bonus Activity

Explore the world of sound design and how sounds are created for movies, games, and music! Ask your teacher or librarian for books or documentaries about sound effects and the role of sound designers in storytelling.
Books:

Other Resources:

Rate This Profession
On a scale of 1 (not interested) to 10 (dream job), how well does this profession suit your personality and interests?

1 2 3 4 5 6 7 8 9 10

87. MAGAZINE EDITOR

A magazine editor oversees the content, quality, and presentation of a magazine. They work with writers, photographers, and designers to produce engaging accurate content for their target audience.

Your Mission – Imagine you're a magazine editor!

Design Your Editorial Vision What type of magazine would you edit—fashion, lifestyle, tech, health, or news?

Design Challenge What tools and technologies would you use? Think about editorial management software, content management systems, and design tools like Adobe Creative Suite.

Editorial Tools What tools would you use—editing software, layout tools, or editorial calendars for tracking deadlines and content?

A Day in the Life What would your day look like—reviewing articles, working with the writing team, collaborating with designers, or overseeing photo shoots?

Dream Magazine Project If you could work on any magazine project, what would it be—launching a new issue, curating a special feature, or managing an editorial team for a major publication?

Skills for Success What skills are important? Strong writing and editing skills, creativity, project management, attention to detail, and the ability to collaborate with a team.

Talk to an Expert "What's the most exciting issue you've ever worked on?" or "How do you ensure content is both engaging and informative for readers?" or "What advice would you give to someone wanting to become a magazine editor?"

Bonus Activity
Explore the world of magazine publishing! Ask your teacher or librarian for books or documentaries about editing, magazine production, and the impact of editors on storytelling and content creation.
Books:

Other Resources:

Rate This Profession
On a scale of 1 (not interested) to 10 (dream job), how well does this profession suit your personality and interests?
1 2 3 4 5 6 7 8 9 10

88. INTERPRETER

An interpreter facilitates communication by converting spoken or sign language between languages in various settings like conferences, courtrooms, and hospitals, ensuring that all parties understand each other clearly and accurately.

> **Your Mission** – Imagine you're an interpreter!
> **Design Your Service** What type of interpretation would you specialize in—simultaneous, consecutive, or sign language?
> **Design Challenge** What tools would you use—interpretive equipment, microphones, or translation apps?
> **Interpretation Tools** Would you use headsets, translation software, or specialized dictionaries?
> **A Day in the Life** What would your day look like—translating for clients, preparing for assignments, or studying new terminology?
> **Dream Project** What event would you want to interpret for—an international summit, a UN conference, or a medical conference?
> **Skills for Success** Key skills: fluency in languages, listening, speaking, cultural understanding, quick thinking, and focus.
> **Talk to an Expert – Interpreter** "What's the most challenging task you've faced?" or "How do you prepare for complex topics?" or "Any advice for aspiring interpreters?"

Bonus Activity
Explore interpretation! Ask your teacher or librarian for books or documentaries about translation and the role of interpreters.
Books:

Other Resources:

> **Rate This Profession**
> On a scale of 1 (not interested) to 10 (dream job), how well does this profession suit your personality and interests?
> 1 2 3 4 5 6 7 8 9 10

89. INVESTMENT SPECIALIST

An investment specialist provides advice and guidance on financial investments, helping clients manage their portfolios to achieve their financial goals. They analyze market trends, evaluate investment opportunities, and make recommendations on stocks, bonds, mutual funds, and other financial products.

Your Mission – Imagine you're an investment specialist!

Design Your Investment Strategy What investments would you focus on—stocks, real estate, retirement funds, or sustainable investments?

Design Challenge What tools would you use—financial analysis software, portfolio management tools, or market research databases?

Investment Tools Would you use financial modeling software, risk assessment tools, or financial news platforms?

A Day in the Life Would you research opportunities, meet clients, analyze data, or advise on risk management?

Dream Project What would your dream project be—creating an investment fund, advising startups, or developing a financial strategy for a corporation?

Skills for Success Key skills: analytical thinking, financial knowledge, attention to detail, client management, market trend analysis, and communication.

Talk to an Expert – Investment Specialist "What's the most rewarding part of your job?" or "How do you stay updated on trends and strategies?" or "Any advice for aspiring investment specialists?"

Bonus Activity

Explore the world of investment strategies! Ask your teacher or librarian for books or documentaries about financial markets, investing, and the role of investment specialists in managing portfolios.

Books:

Other Resources:

Rate This Profession

On a scale of 1 (not interested) to 10 (dream job), how well does this profession suit your personality and interests?

1 2 3 4 5 6 7 8 9 10

90. TECH STARTUP FOUNDER

A tech startup founder is an entrepreneur who creates and leads a new technology-based business. They identify innovative ideas, develop products or services, and build teams to scale the company. Founders manage everything from business strategy to product development, marketing, and securing funding.

Your Mission – Imagine you're a tech startup founder!

Design Your Startup What kind of technology-based startup would you create—an app, a software solution, AI-powered tools, or hardware innovations?

Design Challenge What resources would you use? Think about development platforms, cloud services, and fundraising strategies.

Startup Tools What tools would you use—project management software, programming languages, or product prototyping tools?

A Day in the Life What would your day look like—pitching investors, managing your team, overseeing product development, or developing a business plan and strategy?

Dream Startup Project If you could create any tech startup, what would it be—a game-changing app, an innovative SaaS solution, or a groundbreaking hardware product?

Skills for Success What skills are important—problem-solving, leadership, technical knowledge, communication, financial acumen, adaptability, and ability to think outside the box are key.

Talk to an Expert – Tech Startup Founder Q&A

"What was the biggest challenge you faced when launching your startup?" or "How do you find the right team for your tech startup?" or "What advice would you give to someone wanting to become a tech startup founder?"

Bonus Activity Dive into the world of innovation and entrepreneurship! Ask your teacher or librarian for books or documentaries about tech startups, entrepreneurship, and the journey of founding a tech company.
Books:

Other Resources:

Rate This Profession
On a scale of 1 (not interested) to 10 (dream job), how well does this profession suit your personality and interests?
1   2   3   4   5   6   7   8   9   10

91. INTELLECTUAL PROPERTY ATTORNEY

An intellectual property (IP) attorney specializes in protecting the intellectual property rights of individuals and businesses. They help clients secure patents, trademarks, copyrights and trade secrets ensuring that their innovations, brand identities, and creative works are legally protected.

Your Mission – Imagine you're an intellectual property attorney!

Design Your Legal Focus What type of IP law would you focus on—patents for inventions, trademarks for brand protection, copyrights for creative works, or trade secrets for business confidentiality?

Design Challenge What tools and resources would you use? Think legal databases, IP management software, and patent search tools.

Legal Tools What tools would you use—legal research platforms, trademark search databases, or patent filing systems?

A Day in the Life What would your day look like—advising clients about IP protection, filing patents or trademarks, negotiating licensing agreements, or litigating IP disputes?

Dream IP Case If you could work on any intellectual property case, what would it be—defending a groundbreaking patent, negotiating a high-profile trademark deal, or advising a tech startup to protect their innovations?

Skills for Success What skills are important? Strong legal knowledge, attention to detail, problem-solving, communication skills, and a deep understanding of intellectual property laws are key.

Talk to an Expert – Intellectual Property Attorney Q&A
"What's the most complex IP case you've worked on?" or "How do you stay up to date with changes in IP law?" or "What advice would you give to someone wanting to become an intellectual property attorney?"

Bonus Activity
Ask your teacher or librarian for books or documentaries about copyright, patents, trademarks, and the legal side of protecting innovations.
Books:

Other Resources:

Rate This Profession
On a scale of 1 (not interested) to 10 (dream job), how well does this profession suit your personality and interests?
1   2   3   4   5   6   7   8   9   10

92. AEROSPACE ENGINEER

An aerospace engineer designs, develops, and tests aircraft, spacecraft, satellites, and other systems related to flight and space exploration. They apply principles of aerodynamics, materials science, structural analysis, and propulsion to create safe and efficient vehicles for air and space travel.

Your Mission – Imagine you're an aerospace engineer!

Design Your Aerospace System What would you create—an aircraft, a space vehicle, or a communication satellite?

Design Challenge What tools would you use—CAD software, wind tunnels, or simulation programs?

Aerospace Tools What tools would you use—modeling software, flight simulators, or propulsion testing?

A Day in the Life What would your day involve—designing systems, running simulations, or working on prototypes?

Dream Aerospace Project What project would you tackle—designing a Mars rover, a hypersonic jet, or a new rocket for space tourism?

Skills for Success Knowledge of physics, materials science, and mechanical engineering, plus problem-solving, creativity, attention to detail, and teamwork are key.

Talk to an Expert – Aerospace Engineer Q&A "What's the most exciting project you've worked on?" or "How do you overcome design challenges in aerospace?" or "What advice would you give to aspiring aerospace engineers?"

Bonus Activity

Explore aerospace engineering! Ask your teacher or librarian for books or documentaries about flight, space exploration, and the technology behind aircraft and spacecraft design.

Books:

Other Resources:

Rate This Profession
On a scale of 1 (not interested) to 10 (dream job), how well does this profession suit your personality and interests?

1 2 3 4 5 6 7 8 9 10

93. DATA SCIENTIST

A data scientist analyzes and interprets complex data to help organizations make informed decisions. They use statistical methods, machine learning, and data visualization techniques to uncover trends, patterns, and insights from large datasets across industries like tech, healthcare, finance, and more.

Your Mission – Imagine you're a data scientist!

Design Your Data Project What kind of data would you analyze—customer behavior, healthcare trends, financial data, or environmental data?

Design Challenge What tools and technologies would you use? Think about programming languages (Python, R), data manipulation tools (Pandas, SQL), or machine learning libraries (TensorFlow, Scikit-learn).

Data Science Tools What tools would you use—data analysis platforms, cloud services, or data visualization tools like Tableau or Power BI?

A Day in the Life What would your day look like—cleaning and processing data, building predictive models, or presenting insights to stakeholders?

Dream Data Project If you could work on any data science project, what would it be—predicting disease outbreaks, developing AI for self-driving cars, or analyzing climate change data?

Skills for Success What skills are important? Strong programming skills, knowledge of machine learning algorithms, statistical analysis, data visualization, and problem-solving are key.

Talk to an Expert – Data Scientist Q&A "What's the most interesting dataset you've worked with?" or "How do you approach solving a data problem with limited data?" or "What advice would you give to someone wanting to become a data scientist?"

Bonus Activity

Ask your teacher or librarian for books or documentaries about data analysis, machine learning, and real-world applications of data science.
Books:

Other Resources:

Rate This Profession

On a scale of 1 (not interested) to 10 (dream job), how well does this profession suit your personality and interests?

1   2   3   4   5   6   7   8   9   10

94. BEEKEEPER

A beekeeper manages and cares for honeybee colonies to produce honey, beeswax, and other bee products, as well as pollinating crops. Beekeepers monitor the health of the hives, ensure the bees have adequate resources, and maintain the colony's environment to maximize productivity.

Your Mission – Imagine you're a beekeeper!

Design Your Beekeeping Operation What type of beekeeping would you focus on—commercial honey production, pollination services for farms, or raising bees for conservation?

Design Challenge What tools and equipment would you use? Think about hives, beekeeping suits, smokers, and honey extraction tools.

Beekeeping Tools What tools would you use—apiary management software, hive monitoring sensors, or extraction machines?

A Day in the Life What would your day look like—checking hives, harvesting honey, performing hive maintenance, or educating others about beekeeping?

Dream Beekeeping Project If you could start any beekeeping venture, what would it be—starting a commercial honey business, contributing to bee conservation efforts, or developing innovative beekeeping technologies?

Skills for Success What skills are important? Knowledge of bee behavior, hive management, patience, and an understanding of the environment and agricultural needs are essential.

Talk to an Expert – Beekeeper Q&A

"What's the most rewarding aspect of being a beekeeper?" or "How do you handle challenges like bee diseases or colony collapse?" or "What advice would you give to someone wanting to become a beekeeper?"

Bonus Activity

Search for books or documentaries about bee behavior, hive management, and the importance of bees in ecosystems.

Books:

Other Resources:

Rate This Profession

On a scale of 1 (not interested) to 10 (dream job), how well does this profession suit your personality and interests?

1   2   3   4   5   6   7   8   9   10

95. ANIMAL RIGHTS SPECIALIST

An animal rights specialist advocates for the ethical treatment and protection of animals. Animal rights specialists educate the public, investigate cases of animal cruelty, and influence policies to improve animal welfare.

Your Mission – Imagine you're an animal rights specialist!

Advocacy Focus What issues would you focus on—protecting endangered species, preventing animal cruelty, or promoting ethical treatment in industries like farming and entertainment?

Policy & Awareness Challenge What strategies would you use? Think about legal advocacy, public awareness campaigns, or working with organizations to improve animal welfare laws.

Investigation & Action Tools What tools would you use—research reports, undercover investigations, petitions, or educational programs?

A Day in the Life What would your day look like—researching laws, rescuing mistreated animals, speaking at events, or meeting with lawmakers to advocate for stronger animal protection policies?

Dream Animal Rights Project If you could work on any project, what would it be—banning animal testing, protecting marine life, or establishing new wildlife sanctuaries?

Skills for Success What skills are important? Passion for animal welfare, knowledge of laws and policies, public speaking, research skills, and determination to create change are key.

Talk to an Expert – Animal Rights Specialist Q&A
"What inspired you to become an animal rights specialist?" or "How do you work with governments and organizations to improve animal welfare?" or "What advice would you give to someone wanting to work in animal rights advocacy?"

Bonus Activity
Explore the world of animal rights! Ask your teacher or librarian for books or documentaries about animal welfare, famous activists, or organizations making a difference.
Books:

Other Resources:

Rate This Profession
On a scale of 1 (not interested) to 10 (dream job), how well does this profession suit your personality and interests?
1   2   3   4   5   6   7   8   9   10

96. UX DESIGNER

A UX Designer improves the interaction between users and products by making digital interfaces intuitive and enjoyable. They research user behavior, conduct usability testing, and enhance overall product experience.

Your Mission – Imagine you're a UX designer!

Design Your Digital Product What type of product would you design—a website, a mobile app, or an interactive system for a specific industry like healthcare or education?

Design Challenge What tools and technologies would you use? Think about design software (Sketch, Figma), prototyping tools, or user testing platforms.

UX Tools What tools would you use—wireframing tools, usability testing software, or collaboration platforms for team feedback?

A Day in the Life What would your day look like—conducting user interviews, designing wireframes, testing prototypes, or collaborating with developers and stakeholders?

Dream UX Project If you could work on any UX project, what would it be—creating an innovative mobile app, redesigning a popular website, or designing a user-friendly health monitoring system?

Skills for Success What skills are important? Empathy for users, proficiency in design and prototyping tools, understanding of human-centered design principles, problem-solving, and communication skills are key.

Talk to an Expert – UX Designer Q&A "What's the most challenging aspect of designing a great user experience?" or "How do you incorporate user feedback into your design process?" or "What advice would you give to someone wanting to become a UX designer?"

Bonus Activity

Search for books or documentaries about user experience, design thinking, and the impact of design on user interactions.

Books:

Other Resources:

Rate This Profession
On a scale of 1 (not interested) to 10 (dream job), how well does this profession suit your personality and interests?
1   2   3   4   5   6   7   8   9   10

97. CLIMATE CHANGE ANALYST

A climate change analyst studies the impacts of climate change on the environment and society. They analyze data, create models for future scenarios, and develop strategies for mitigation and adaptation. They often collaborate with governments, research organizations, and environmental agencies.

    Your Mission – Imagine you're a climate change analyst!
    Research Focus What aspect of climate change would you focus on—carbon emissions, renewable energy, or climate policies?
    Tools & Tech: What tools would you use—data analysis software, climate models, or GIS for mapping changes?
    A Day in the Life What would your day look like—gathering data, analyzing trends, or advising on strategies?
    Dream Project If you could work on any project, what would it be—developing global policies, designing sustainable cities, or creating an educational campaign?
    Skills for Success Analytical skills, environmental science knowledge, data interpretation, and problem-solving.
    Talk to an Expert "What's the most significant climate trend you've observed?" or "How do you stay updated on climate science?" or "What advice would you give to an aspiring climate change analyst?"

Bonus Activity:
Explore climate change and sustainability! Ask your teacher or librarian for books or documentaries on climate impacts, renewable energy, and global policies.
Books:

Other Resources:

Rate This Profession
On a scale of 1 (not interested) to 10 (dream job), how well does this profession suit your personality and interests?
1 2 3 4 5 6 7 8 9 10

98. GENETIC COUNSELOR

A genetic counselor provides guidance and support to individuals or families regarding genetic conditions. They interpret genetic test results, assess risk factors, and help people understand how genetics may affect their health, family planning, or future generations. Genetic counselors also offer emotional support and help clients make informed decisions.

Your Mission Imagine you're a genetic counselor!
Design Your Counseling Approach What type of genetic counseling would you focus on—preconception, prenatal, cancer genetics, or rare genetic disorders?
Design Challenge What tools and technologies would you use? Think about genetic testing software, family history tools, or genetic databases.
Genetic Tools What tools would you use—genetic analysis platforms, educational resources or counseling software for documentation?
A Day in the Life What would your day look like—meeting with clients, interpreting test results, providing guidance on health risks, or researching new genetic advancements?
Dream Genetic Counseling Project If you could work on any genetic counseling project, what would it be—helping a family understand a rare genetic disorder, supporting patients with cancer risk, or working on genetic testing innovations?
Skills for Success What skills are important? Strong communication, empathy, knowledge of genetics, critical thinking, and the ability to explain complex medical concepts clearly are essential.
Talk to an Expert – Genetic Counselor Q&A "What's the best part of your job?" or "How do you keep up with genetic advancements?" or "Any advice for future genetic counselors?"

Bonus Activity
Explore books or documentaries on genetic disorders, testing, or counseling.
Books:

Other Resources:

Rate This Profession
On a scale of 1 (not interested) to 10 (dream job), how well does this profession suit your personality and interests?
1 2 3 4 5 6 7 8 9 10

99. SMART HOME DESIGNER

A smart home designer specializes in creating and implementing integrated technology systems within homes to enhance convenience, security, energy efficiency, and comfort. They design systems that control lighting, temperature, entertainment, and security through voice commands, apps, or automated schedules, making homes more intelligent and responsive to the needs of their residents.

Your Mission – Imagine you're a smart home designer!

Design Your Smart Home System What features would you focus on—automated lighting, smart security, climate control, or entertainment systems?

Design Challenge What tools and technologies would you use—smart devices, home automation platforms, or IoT systems?

Smart Home Tools What tools would you use—control hubs, energy management systems, or system integration software?

A Day in the Life What would your day look like—consulting with clients, designing systems, testing devices, or troubleshooting installations?

Dream Smart Home Project If you could work on any project, what would it be—designing a fully automated sustainable home, creating a home that adapts to residents' needs, or developing systems for elderly care?

Skills for Success Knowledge of home automation, electrical wiring, problem-solving, design skills, and understanding IoT devices.

Talk to an Expert – Smart Home Designer Q&A

"What's the most exciting part of designing smart homes?" or "How do you ensure seamless integration between devices?" or "What advice would you give to aspiring smart home designers?"

Bonus Activity: Explore smart home tech! Ask your teacher or librarian for books or documentaries on home automation, smart devices, and the future of interconnected living.

Books:

Other Resources:

Rate This Profession

On a scale of 1 (not interested) to 10 (dream job), how well does this profession suit your personality and interests?

1   2   3   4   5   6   7   8   9   10

100. EDUCATIONAL CONSULTANT

An educational consultant provides expert advice to students, parents, schools, or educational organizations on various educational matters. They may help with curriculum design, college admissions, special education strategies, or the implementation of new learning technologies.

Your Mission – Imagine you're an educational consultant!

Design Your Services What type of educational consulting would you focus on—curriculum development, student assessment, or school leadership?

Design Challenge What tools and technologies would you use—data analysis software, learning management systems, or educational research?

Consulting Tools What tools would you use—assessment tools, teacher training materials, or educational resources?

A Day in the Life What would your day look like—working with schools, researching educational trends, or advising on teaching strategies?

Dream Project If you could work on any project, what would it be—designing a new teaching program, improving student outcomes, or developing a technology-based learning initiative?

Skills for Success Knowledge of education systems, problem-solving, communication, data analysis, and expertise in curriculum design.

Talk to an Expert – Educational Consultant Q&A

"What's the most rewarding part of being an educational consultant?" or "How do you stay updated on the latest educational trends?" or "What advice would you give to someone wanting to become an educational consultant?"

Bonus Activity:
Ask your teacher or librarian for books or documentaries about curriculum development, educational trends, and innovative teaching strategies.
Books:

Other Resources:

Rate This Profession
On a scale of 1 (not interested) to 10 (dream job),
how well does this profession suit your personality and interests?
1   2   3   4   5   6   7   8   9   10

101. AUDITOR

An auditor is a professional who examines financial records, accounts, and business practices to ensure accuracy, compliance with regulations, and efficiency. They assess internal controls, identify discrepancies and provide recommendations for improvements. Auditors work in various industries, including public accounting firms, corporations, and government agencies.

Your Mission – Imagine you're an auditor!

Design Your Audit Focus What area would you specialize in—financial audits, compliance audits, or internal control reviews?

Design Challenge What tools and technologies would you use—audit software, financial analysis tools, or data visualization programs?

Audit Tools What tools would you use—accounting software, spreadsheets, or risk assessment tools?

A Day in the Life What would your day look like—examining financial statements, conducting interviews, analyzing data, or preparing reports?

Dream Project If you could work on any audit project, what would it be—conducting a forensic audit, ensuring compliance for a major corporation, or improving internal controls for a nonprofit?

Skills for Success Strong analytical skills, attention to detail, knowledge of accounting principles, communication, and problem-solving.

Talk to an Expert – Auditor Q&A

"What's the most challenging audit you've worked on?" or "How do you ensure accuracy and compliance during an audit?" or "What advice would you give to someone wanting to become an auditor?"

Bonus Activity:
Explore the world of auditing! Ask your teacher or librarian for books or documentaries about financial auditing, risk management, and the role of auditors in business.
Books:

Other Resources:

Rate This Profession
On a scale of 1 (not interested) to 10 (dream job), how well does this profession suit your personality and interests?
1   2   3   4   5   6   7   8   9   10

So Many Cool Jobs Out There!

What we've covered, randomly listed jobs, is just a glimpse into the vast world of careers. There are hundreds of unique jobs—and the list keeps growing! Every year, new and exciting careers emerge that no one ever imagined before!

Jobs change fast. In a few years, there could be robots driving cars or helping people translate languages. Maybe in the future there won't be need for human drivers anymore, or a robot could be your personal assistant you help you find answers to questions! Technology is moving super quickly, and we can only imagine how cool jobs will look in the future.

The best part? You can be ready for whatever job you dream of by learning new skills and exploring all kinds of interests. The more things you know, the better prepared you'll be for anything that comes your way. Whether you want to create the next coolest video game, build a flying car, or discover ways to help the planet, there's a job for it!

So, don't just focus on one thing. Try new hobbies, read books about careers, or ask adults about their jobs. Every time you learn something new you're adding to your superpowers to help you in the future. You never know where your interests will take you. The job you've never heard of yet could be the perfect fit for you!

The Gift of Possibility

Every day brings new opportunities. They could be big or small and if you keep your eyes open, you'll notice them. Maybe you'll meet someone who shares your passion for animals or discover a new hobby you never thought about before. Being open to possibilities means giving yourself the chance to grow in ways you never imagined.

That same spirit of openness applies to your future career. The world is changing fast, and with every new invention or discovery, new jobs are born. If you're fascinated by technology and the future, you could explore futuristic careers like memory implant specialist, dream augmentation specialist, or even interplanetary lawyer. These professions might sound like science fiction today, but they could be part of your reality tomorrow.

But even if the cutting edge of technology isn't your thing, the beauty of possibility is that it stretches in every direction. If you love creativity and design, there are so many paths that connect. Maybe you see yourself as an artist, but you could also be a graphic designer, a toy designer, or a fashion designer. Creativity doesn't fit into just one box—it flows into unexpected places, like designing interactive virtual worlds, shaping sustainable homes, or even helping brands tell their stories in powerful ways.

The key is to see your interests not as isolated points, but as part of a web of possibilities. Each talent you develop, each curiosity you follow opens doors to something else. Maybe your passion for animals connects to your desire to be a veterinarian, but perhaps also a wildlife photographer, marine biologist, or even a toy designer creating eco-friendly animal toys for kids.

You don't have to choose just one thing and stick with it forever. The world is too big, and you are too full of potential. Whether you lean toward the high-tech, the creative, or the hands-on professions, there are always adjacent paths—careers that borrow skills from each other and give you new ways to use what you love.

You don't have to figure everything out right now—just keep an open heart and mind, and the world will keep offering you incredible experiences. The gift of possibility is always there, waiting for you to unwrap it.

Find Your Purpose and Keep Going – Japanese Secrets to Stay Motivated

Have you ever wondered why some people always seem to have endless energy and never give up on their goals? They wake up excited every day, ready to take on new challenges and chase their dreams. It's like they've discovered the secret to staying motivated!

Some of the most powerful secrets come from Japan. They can help you find purpose and stay motivated too. Want to know how?

Let's start with a cool idea called **Ikigai**. This word means "a reason to wake up in the morning." In Japan, it's all about finding something that makes you excited and happy to do. It's like a treasure hunt for your life's purpose! Ikigai is the sweet spot where four important things meet: what you love, what you're good at, what the world needs, and what you can be paid to do. Imagine if you could find something you enjoy, you're good at, helps others, and even helps you earn money! That's the dream, right? So, think about what makes you happy, what you're passionate about, and where they could overlap in your future.

Next, there's **Kaizen**. This word means "continuous improvement," where you get a little bit better every day. No matter what you're working on—school, hobbies, or learning new skills, kaizen helps you grow step by step. It's okay to make mistakes, but the most important thing is to keep trying and improving every day. You don't need to be perfect right away. The secret is doing a little better than yesterday, no matter how small the step. If you do this, you'll keep growing and getting closer to your goals every day.

Now, let's talk about a technique called the **Pomodoro Technique**. It's a fun way to stay focused and get things done! Here's how it works: You set a timer for 25 minutes and focus completely on a task. After 25 minutes, take a 5-minute break! Repeat this until you've done a few rounds, and then take a longer break. This helps you stay sharp and not get too tired while working. It's like a fun game where you try to beat the timer, and it helps you stay on track without feeling burned out!

Another cool Japanese idea is **Shoshin**, which means "beginner's mind." This reminds you to always stay curious and open to learning, no matter how much you already know. When you have a beginner's mind, you approach everything with fresh eyes and excitement, even if you've done it before. It's like looking at the world with wonder, ready to discover something new! This can help you stay motivated and inspired when things get tough. When you approach every challenge with curiosity, you open yourself up to new possibilities and exciting opportunities!

Finally, there's the idea of **Wabi-sabi**. It's the art of seeing beauty in imperfections. Life isn't always perfect, and neither are we. Wabi-sabi teaches us to appreciate the little things, even the mistakes. It helps us realize that life's challenges and struggles are what make us unique and strong. So, when things don't go as planned, don't be discouraged! Embrace the journey, learn from your mistakes, and celebrate your growth. Every moment, even the tough ones, is a chance to learn and grow.

So, how can you use all these ideas to find your purpose and stay motivated? Think about what makes you excited, just like Ikigai. Keep improving a little every day with Kaizen. Use the Pomodoro technique to focus and get things done. Stay curious and open to learning with Shoshin and embrace life's imperfections with Wabi-sabi. These powerful tools will help you keep going, even when things feel tough, and will guide you toward finding your true purpose. Just remember it's all about taking small steps, staying positive, and believing in yourself! You've got this!

What If I Still Choose the Wrong Profession?

Focus on what you like and keep moving forward! It's completely normal to wonder, "What if I don't like my choice of profession?" You might worry that once you've picked something, you're stuck with it forever. But here's the thing: it's never too late to change course.

Life is full of twists and turns, and what you might love today could evolve as you learn more about yourself. It's part of growing! The good news is that by the time you realize a profession doesn't suit you, you already have valuable insights into what you truly enjoy and what excites you. You're closer to figuring out your perfect fit than you might think!

Take comfort in the fact that knowing what you don't like can be just as important as knowing what you do like. It means you've learned something about your preferences, strengths, and where you feel happiest and most fulfilled. The key is not to stay stuck in a situation that doesn't feel right, but to take that knowledge and use it to make a change.

Imagine your perfect job, where you wake up feeling excited for the day ahead. It's about the right people and the right environment. A job with supportive colleagues in a positive workplace can make all the difference in how you feel every day.

Remember, finding the right job and career path is like finding the right pair of shoes—you have to try a few to discover which ones fit perfectly. Once you find the right profession, everything else falls into place. You'll feel happier, more accomplished, and ready to tackle the world!

So, if you ever find yourself thinking that your current choice isn't the best fit, don't worry. It's all part of the journey. The right job, the right people, and the right environment can make your everyday life much more enjoyable and fulfilling. Keep exploring, stay open to new opportunities, and trust that the right path will unfold for you!

Skills, Skills, and More Skills!

We live in a fast-changing world where professions are constantly evolving, sometimes faster than we can keep up with. That's why developing new skills is essential for keeping up with the times and unlocking exciting new opportunities. No matter what career you choose, one thing is clear: lifelong learning is the key to success.

Take teaching, for example. In the past teachers worked without any technology at all — not a single gadget in sight! Lessons were taught with chalk on blackboards, textbooks were our only source of knowledge, and homework was written by hand. That was it. But fast forward to today, and classrooms are packed with technology — interactive smart boards, online platforms for homework, educational apps, and even virtual reality lessons in some schools. Modern teachers need to know it all, from managing online classrooms to using digital tools to make learning fun and effective.

Rapid changes are reshaping nearly every profession. Jobs that once required hands-on skills or in-person interaction now rely on digital tools, remote communication, and new technologies. The COVID-19 pandemic highlighted the importance of online communication, moving school, work, and social activities online. Virtual meetings, online tutoring, and remote learning are now the norm, and they're here to stay. Today, most young people have taken at least one online class, and many jobs expect remote work and online collaboration skills.

New technologies, new ways of working, and even entirely new professions will continue to appear, and each one brings new growth opportunities. Whether it's mastering a new app, learning how to code, improving your public speaking, or discovering creative problem-solving techniques, every new skill you add becomes part of your personal toolkit. The more skills you have, the more adaptable you'll be — ready to take on new challenges, switch careers if needed, or even create your own path.

The world will keep changing, but that's what makes it exciting! As long as you keep learning, stay curious, and believe in your ability to adapt, you'll be ready for anything the future brings — and you'll never stop discovering just how capable you really are.

Dream Big and You will Change the World!

You have the power to change the world! Seriously—you do! It might sound like a huge dream, but it's absolutely possible when you bring your creativity, curiosity, and unique talents into the world. Every skill you learn, every idea you share, and every passion you follow can create ripples of positive change. And guess what helps you do that? Choosing the right profession—the one that fits who you are and what you care about most.

Your profession isn't just about having a job or earning money. It's about discovering a path where you get to shine—where your talents, imagination, and energy can make a real difference. Whether you're drawn to creating art, solving scientific mysteries, teaching kids, healing others, or building the future, every profession holds the power to make life better for someone, somewhere.

Think about it! When you combine your skills, knowledge, and the special spark only you have, you're not just working—you're helping shape a better world. Artists bring beauty and new ideas to life. Doctors and scientists save lives and uncover solutions to big problems. Engineers build safer cities. Teachers spark curiosity that lasts a lifetime. Every profession has the power to make life brighter, easier, or more inspiring for someone.

And the best part? Change doesn't always come from giant, world-shaking events. It can come from you—the way you approach your work, the way you care, and the ideas you share. Maybe you'll invent something groundbreaking. Maybe you'll create something beautiful that inspires millions. Or maybe you'll be the one who helps others believe in themselves for the first time. No matter what you choose, you have the potential to make every day a little better, for yourself and for others.

So, as you explore all the incredible professions out there, remember this: **Your profession is your superpower.** It's how you turn your ideas into reality, your passion into action, and your dreams into something the whole world can see and feel. Keep believing in yourself and dreaming big—because you absolutely can change the world, just by doing what you love.

Your Dream Profession – The Ultimate Checklist

So, you've been thinking about your future, exploring different careers, and discovering what excites you the most. Now it's time for the final step: using a checklist to help you decide your dream profession! This checklist will guide you as you narrow your options to find that perfect fit for you. Ready to take a look?

The Ultimate Checklist – Is This Your Dream Job?
1. Do I Enjoy This?
    - Are you excited about this job?
    - Is it something you could happily spend your time doing?
2. Am I Good at It?
    - Do you have the skills or talent for this career?
    - Are you willing to practice and improve?
3. Will It Make Me Proud?
    - Will this job make you feel like you're helping others or making a difference?
    - Does it align with your values and what you want to achieve?
4. Is It Fun or Interesting?
    - Does it make you curious and eager to learn more?
    - Will you look forward to challenges and problem-solving?
5. Can I Be Creative or Use My Strengths?
    - Will this career allow you to use your imagination, creativity, or special skills?
    - Does it let you express your personality in the work you do?
6. Will I Be Able to Work with Others?
    - Do you like the idea of working with others and being part of a team?
    - Are you comfortable communicating and collaborating?
7. Can I See Myself Doing It for a Long Time?
    - Does this job excite you, not just today, but in the future as well?
    - Can you picture yourself in this profession for years to come?
8. Does It Match My Interests and Passions?
    - Does the job fit what you enjoy doing in your free time?
    - Does it connect with your hobbies, interests, or subjects you love to learn about?
9. Will It Allow Me to Grow?
    - Does this career offer opportunities to learn new things and improve over time?

- Is there room for you to grow and get better in the job?
10. Does It Help Me Achieve My Goals?
    - Will this job help you reach your personal and professional goals in the long run?
    - Will it give provide a sense of accomplishment and success?

Take a moment to look over these questions and think about the jobs you're interested in. Does the career you're considering check off most (or all!) of these boxes? If it does, then you're on the right track toward finding your dream profession!

Remember, there's no rush—figuring out what you want to do with your life takes time. And, if you find out later that something isn't the right fit, that's okay too! You can always try new things, learn more about yourself, and keep exploring.

Your Turn: Use the Checklist!
Now that you have your checklist, grab a pencil and circle the jobs that excite you. Write down the ones seem to fit you best and why. Remember, this is your journey, and it's okay to change direction or explore new options as you grow!

Your dream job is out there, and with the right questions and a bit of guidance, you're getting closer to finding it.

Keep exploring, until you find your perfect fit!

www.ingramcontent.com/pod-product-compliance
Lightning Source LLC
Chambersburg PA
CBHW060157050426
42446CB00013B/2863